Prairie Flower

PRAIRIE FLOWER, machine appliquéd by Jean Stanclift, Lawrence, Kan.; machine quilted by Rosie Mayhew, Topeka, Kan. (See page 75.)

Prairie Flower

A Year on the Plains

Barbara Brackman

Prairie Flower
A Year on the Plains
New Appliqué Patterns in
The Kansas City Star Heritage

Author: Barbara Brackman
Editors: Doug Weaver and Sue Spade
Design: Sue Spade
Illustrations: Barbara Brackman
and Peter Cole
Template illustrations: Gentry Mullen
Photography: Susan Pfannmuller,
Tim Janicke and Jim Barcus

Published by

KANSAS CITY STAR BOOKS
1729 Grand Blvd.
Kansas City, Missouri, USA 64108

First edition, first printing
Library of Congress Control Number:
2001093881
ISBN: 0-9712920-0-0

Printed in the United States of America
by Walsworth Publishing Co.,
Marceline, Mo.

To order copies, call StarInfo at
(816) 234-4636 and say "BOOKS."
Or order on-line at www.PickleDish.com.

Cover quilt detail and quilt on page 24 are
Prairie Flower Journal by Kathy Delaney,
Overland Park, Kan. Quilted by Charlotte
Gurwell, 2001

ABOUT THE AUTHOR

BARBARA BRACKMAN began collecting quilt patterns when she found a package of Kansas City Star clippings in a thrift store in 1965. Since then, collecting and organizing patterns has been one of her major interests. She has published several books on quilts including "Encyclopedia of Pieced Quilt Patterns" and "Encyclopedia of Appliqué." She has also adapted pattern indexes to computers with BlockBase and her new program Create Your Family Quilt Using State Blocks and Symbols.

Barbara was born in New York City and went to high school in the Kansas City area. She moved to Lawrence, Kan., to attend the University of Kansas and has lived there since. She consults for numerous museums including the Kansas Museum of History, the Kansas City Museum and the Spencer Museum at the University of Kansas. The Prairie Flower Project grew out of her long-term interest in women's history.

Table of Contents

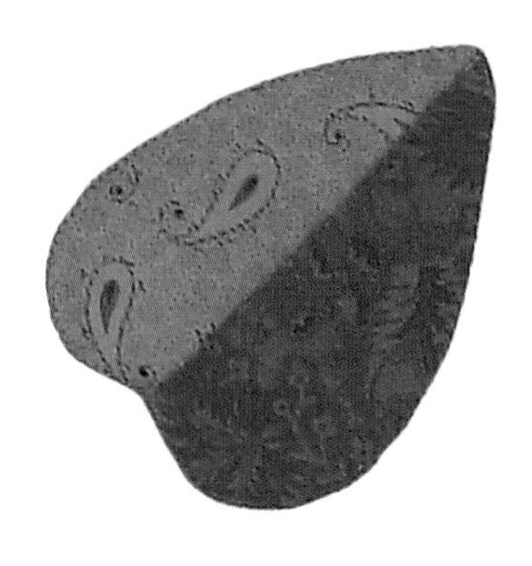

Introduction

Quilts are entwined with America's pioneer heritage. We take great pride in our westering spirit. Quilts, so distinctly American, seem a part of the frontier experience. The Prairie Flower Project combines a view of women's Western migration with new quilt design based on the wildflowers of the great plains.

The project originally was published as a series of 12 monthly blocks in *The Kansas City Star* during the year 2001. Each floral block is an original pattern, based on principles of traditional applique design. I planned the blocks with the four-way symmetrical repeat so common in 19th-century floral quilts. The flowers, drawn from nature, are composed of simple shapes typical in antique applique. I chose wildflowers described in the diaries, letters and memoirs of pioneering women and girls. When possible, the block was published in the month during which it blooms, giving the quiltmaker a view of a year on the plains.

Prairie women and their handwork. The Ladies' Aid Society, Elk, Chase County, Kansas, about 1900. Courtesy of Kansas State Historical Society.

Their words about wildflowers give us a glimpse of women's view of their new home. I've always enjoyed reading their first reactions to the prairie landscape. Like them, I came from the East with little idea of what to expect. Born in New York City and raised in Cincinnati, I recall my anxieties as a 13-year-old moving to a place called Prairie Village.

I didn't understand that it was a Kansas City suburb. I expected a yard full of sand with deer and antelope playing. Although reassured by newly laid sod and the Blue Spruce tree near the front door of our new ranch house, I spent years getting used to a landscape with horizon on all sides. Fortunately, I was well schooled by friends who are native Kansans. They taught me to love the landscape, the botany underfoot and the seasonal subtleties in color and weather.

Prairie women and quilting

*"**I** botanize and read some but cook a 'heap' more."*
— Letter from Tamsen Donner, June 16, 1846.

MANY OF THE WOMEN encountering the prairie 150 years ago were passing through, bound for other Western places, especially Oregon and California. Some were long-term visitors, wives of army officers or government officials, living on the frontier for a year or two. And many came as permanent settlers, like Sara Robinson, whose husband became the first governor of Kansas, or Luna Warner, who grew up on the prairie.

ALTHOUGH THIS PHOTO was taken in 1908 in Johnson County, Kan., it shows a typical horse and wagon outfit that might have been used for shorter trips in the previous century. Cross-country travelers used oxen rather than horses to pull their wagons. Courtesy of Kansas State Historical Society.

Each of these women looked at wild flowers in different ways. Unusual species were part of the adventure. Familiar flowers provided a link to home. The wild flowers that thrived on the plains often served as compensation for fussier types that couldn't be cultivated in their gardens.

Most travelers crossed the western border of the United States into Indian Territory in early May. At that point the grass was deep enough to feed the oxen that pulled their wagons and the horses, cows and other livestock they brought along. After the pioneers left the world of steamboats, trains and stage coaches, their pace slowed to about 15 to 20 miles per day. Parties that left too late in May risked being stranded in the snowy mountains in the fall. Parties that left too early couldn't find forage for the animals.

May is the season when the prairie is at its worst and its best. The skies roll with thunderclouds, winds whip across the hills and curl into tornadoes, poisonous snakes and scorpions awake from winter naps, streams overflow and the path worn by hundreds of wagons turns to muck. Yet the new grass is awash with wild flowers. The air is crisp and the sun offers a welcoming warmth in a chilly morning. It is

"CYCLONE AT KESWICK (Iowa). Edna Horn sitting on the cook stove." About 1890.

no wonder that the Western vistas impressed the newcomers.

Women steaming west on the Missouri River or walking across Iowa or Missouri knew they were heading to a different landscape. The prairie was, to people of European roots, a strange wide space with no significant mountains, lakes or oceans to define its edges. Some, like Elizabeth Ann Cooley, on a Missouri River steamboat in 1846, eagerly looked for a new experience. *"Almost to Independence....Passed Lexington and Camden yesterday evening...saw a fair wide beautiful prairie for the first time."*

Many of the women were young, often newly married, glad of an adventure and a break with the past. Elizabeth Keegan's enthusiasm rings in her letters back home. *"But I must first tell you something of the route. The first part of it is beautiful and the scenery surpassing anything of the kind I have ever seen ... large rolling prairies stretching as far as your eye can carry you covered with verdure. The grass so green and flowers of every description from violets to geraniums of richest hue."*

Many compared the treeless expanse to the small patches of grassland they knew – a park, a cultivated lawn or meadow. But the Platte River, the wide, shallow, muddy Platte that etched the road west across the Great Plains, defied comparison to Eastern waterways. Martha Missouri Moore described it as *"a perfect curiosity, it is so different from our own streams that it is hard to realize that river should be running so near the top of the ground without any timber and in no bank at all."*

Some women stepped only anxiously past the edge of what they saw as "civilization." Like Sara Robinson, they had read as school girls of the Great American Desert, a wild and savage country inhospitable to humans except for the nomadic Natives. But to most, like Abigail Scott Duniway, the land west of Missouri was a pleasant surprise. *"The country as we pass along, looks more and more level; and the plains certainly wear a charm which I little expected to see...the little hollows which at a short distance from the road we can see at almost any time are generally filled with flowers and veregated with ten thousand tints..."*

Far more frightening than the vistas were the snakes, wolves and coyotes, plus the human inhabitants with their strange culture and painted faces. Helen

"We were now fairly launched on the waving prairie. A person who has beheld neither the ocean nor the great, silent, uninhabited plains, will find it impossible to form any adequate idea of the grandeur of the scene..."

— Julia Archibald Holmes, 1858

Carpenter on her way to Oregon described her ambivalence about leaving the Kansas Territory. *"This is certainly the most beautiful country. The grass is from one to ten feet high, and there is a profusion of wild flowers all over the prairie. But the violent thunder storms are enough to wreck the nerves of Hercules and the rattlesnakes are as thick as the leaves on the trees."*

THE WOMAN IN the wheelchair with the impressive bouquet is identified as Vice President Charles Curtis's cousin, who was deaf from childhood. Probably Topeka. About 1940.

•

Helen was among the many women who took the time to mention the wildflowers she encountered. She liked to "botanize," to use Tamsen Donner's word, meaning she kept her eyes open for new plants, made lists of what she saw, compared them to those she knew in the East and picked them to beautify her campsite. Susan Magoffin, traveling the Santa Fe Trail, had the same kind of curiosity. *"Many a one of these long hills do I walk up and down, besides rambling through the bushes, along the banks of the little streams &c. in search of 'what I can find.' Some times this is a curious little pebble, a shell, a new flower, or the quill of a strange bird."*

•

THE WOMAN in the picture loved to "botanize." On the reverse of the photo wrote, "Owen and me. On the desert in El Centro, California, 1926. Hot. We are looking at a cactus blossom altho' it don't look like I am. My hand is just above his. The Cactus bloom is a bright red one of a cone shape. The top of the bush which can be seen is full of red cones."

Marriett Foster Cummings kept careful track of what she found.

"June 13 1852. Saw a new flower, the Lily of the Black Hills.

"June 15 Gresewood and sage have been abundant for a few days....Saw two species of cactus in bloom and a new flower a little resembling the pink, but without a fragrance."

Elizabeth Crawford wrote home of the familiar species. *"You wish me to tell you the names of some of our wild woods flowers. There is the wild sweet william, wild pink, lady slipper, wild roses, butterfly weed, wild honey suckle, blue flag, yellow flag and there is a great many other kinds, that I can't recall the names of at this time."*

CHILDREN UNDER the climbing gardens in a farmyard. About 1900.

Unfamiliar species usually inspired enthusiasm. Elizabeth Myrick found the cactus stunning in what is now western Nebraska, a country so devoid of trees that campfires were made of dried buffalo dung. *"Camped on the Platte this evening the boys gathered buffalo chips the plains abound in the most beautiful wild flower I ever seen....your garden flowers in the States would envy them for their beauty The Turkish crown is a species of the Prickly Pear only it is of a more beautiful form and has a pink and yellow flower on it."*

Lissie Butler Hutchinson, however, was not enchanted with the Western landscape she encountered on her trip to a new home in the Oregon woods.

In a letter to her niece back in New Hampshire, she expressed her homesickness in terms of what she lacked. *"Lavinia I want you to go to that little hickory grove on the west of the old home and pick two of the nicest oak leaves you can find and send them in your next letter also two hickory ones at different times along. I wish you would continue to send until you send every kind of leaf that grows in the old granate State. Send me a leaf off Gran Ma's favorite walnut also one off the rose bush by the front door."*

"MYRT GREENFIELD and husband." Mr. Greenfield appears to be a peace officer. They've cultivated hollyhocks on the left, a climbing vine on the right and some potted plants on the porch. About 1925.

As the pioneers settled into Western homes, their flower gardens came to reflect their new sense of place. While some like Sara Robinson transplanted wildflowers into their yards, others planted the cultivated species they'd brought with them. Emily Combes described the claim she homesteaded with her father in Rice County, Kan. *"The little sod house, with its little square window is nearly covered with vines ... a pumpkin vine ... the huge yellow blooms look like golden trumpets. The floor of the house is dirt but as dry and hard as cement. We have sprinkled it with water and pounded it with a maul so as to make it hard and smooth as possible. On it are rugs made of coffee sacks."*

•

"This week our route has been over a rolling prairie beautiful to behold. We frequently see wolves or those who guard do and 7 rattle snakes have been seen by the Co. since we started. We find Leeach lillies and star of Bethlehem wild here. Wagon run over Mrs Bryant's foot."

— Celinda Hines, May 21, 1853

Over time, women settlers traded leaves, seeds and pressed flowers with family in the States, and their prairie gardens grew to be more like those they left behind. Wrote Sarah Everett: *"Have the seeds I sent you come up? Mine are up and doing nicely. My flowers as a whole do first rate, some kinds the soil does not seem to agree with, but most of them do look nicely. I have...morning glories planted in a circle with a stick in the middle & strings run from the circle to the top."*

CORA M. LUBY and her morning glories. About 1910.

Cultivated roses and peonies and hybridized lilacs and hydrangeas came to the plains with lace curtains, bone china and carpet that replaced coffee sacks over dirt floors. Flower gardens behind fences symbolized the conquering of the West. Women who took pride in their ability to "civilize" the prairie forgot about sorrel, sweet william, and johnny-jump-ups. Today, however, we once again look to native species for our contemporary gardens, realizing that rudbeckia and columbine are easier to raise than rhododendron and roses. As we once again transplant wildflowers, we can imagine the pleasure they gave to the pioneers.

•

It would be nice to think that the prairie flowers inspired the pioneer women to make quilts, but there is little evidence of any kind of quiltmaking on the frontier. Women traveling across the plains or making new homes on farms and in towns haven't left us quilts and comforters. The pioneering women didn't seem to make even simple pieced work quilts for warmth, much less fancy applique florals for special. When I worked on the Kansas Quilt Project team in the 1980s, we recorded information about quilts in private collections, hoping to document quilts made on the Kansas frontier in the 1850s and '60s. In those decades women "back in the states" were stitching masterpiece quilts of applique and stuffed work, silk and imported French cottons. We wondered what kinds of quilts came from the hands of women settling the Western frontier. Would they be of the same kinds of imported fabrics; feature the same fine needlework? To our surprise, we found no examples of quilts reliably accounted to have been made in Kansas before the 1870s. Women settling into new lives on the edge of the frontier did not make quilts.

"I got out and took a ramble. I picked numberless flowers with which the plains are covered, and as [my husband] told me before we started, I threw them away to gather more."

— Susan Shelby Mogoffin, June 12, 1846, near Black Jack, 49 miles west of Independence.

A BABY, a silk puff quilt, a goat skin rug, a potted geranium and a coleus in Oregon. About 1900.

After much thought, we decided that the reason must be that women brought their quilts with them. They couldn't bring much. They were advised to bring cookware and bedding, leaving their stoves and beds behind. We found that many families had heirloom quilts made in the East and brought to Kansas in the mid 19th century. Some were slept under and worn, many undoubtedly slept under and worn out, but quite a few were passed down through the generations in nearly unused condition.

The quilts in so many Kansas and Missouri homes are much surviving evidence of the importance of these quilts to the families settling the frontier and their descendents.

"A GLIMPSE OF THE HOMESTEAD." The idealized farm from a Currier and Ives print in 1865.

SPINDLY TREES just older than seedlings and a hardy vegetable garden add only a touch of the eastern landscape to the Anderson's farm in Logan County, Kan., about 1890. Courtesy of Kansas State Historical Society.

How to Machine Appliqué

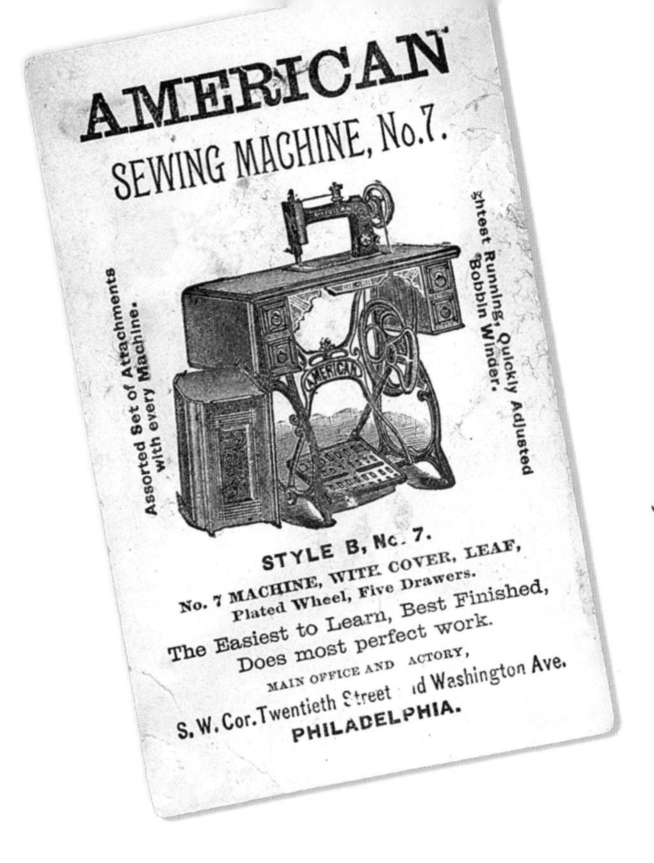

PRACTICAL TIPS FOR FAST, ACCURATE PATCHWORK

JEAN STANCLIFT appliquéd our sample quilt using a machine technique she has really mastered. Jean and her friends Karla Menaugh and Cherie Ralston have been perfecting their invisible machine appliqué techniques by adapting ideas from several teachers.

Over fifteen years ago *Quilters' Newsletter Magazine* described the basics of appliquéing with a blind hemstitch in an article by Jeri Hoffmeyer and Marie Shirer. They suggested the appliqué pieces be backed with a fusible interfacing, but our technique uses freezer paper. We are enthusiastic about this machine appliqué that looks like hand appliqué. It goes quickly, but the real advantage is the accuracy. I have never been much of an appliqué artist, but I can do a decent job using freezer paper and the machine.

FABRIC REQUIREMENTS

Backgrounds

A glance at the quilts scattered throughout the book reveals the wide variety of styles possible through fabric choice. Several of the quilts have a contemporary look with dark backgrounds and florals cut from the bright fabrics that look hand-dyed. Others are more traditional with light-colored backgrounds and flowers of soft calicoes. A few feature a mix-and-match background with different prints in similar shades behind the appliqué. This trick gives a definite contemporary shading to traditional design

Decide on your color scheme — dramatic or romantic, dark or pastel, figured floral prints or swirly batiks. The blocks are cut 19" square and then trimmed to 18 1/2". You can get two blocks out of every 20" of fabric. If you want all 12 blocks to have the same background, multiply 20" times six and buy 120" (3 1/2 yards) of fabric. If you want to mix and match your backgrounds, find three coordinating backgrounds and get 40" of each (about 1 1/4 yards). Or try six different backgrounds buying 2/3 of a yard each.

But wait! Don't shop yet because you

still have to calculate the border yardage. It's best to buy all the fabric at the same time. See page 79 for four border ideas and yardages.

The Flowers

Wild flowers bloom in a variety of shades all around the color wheel.

You'll need scraps of many shades. If you haven't enough in your scrap bag – or want to buy something new – buy fat quarters. Leaf through the book and study the blocks. You'll need a minimum of 3 or 4 purples, light to dark; 3 or 4 yellows to gold; 2 or 3 oranges and 2 pinks. Wildflowers rarely appear in greens or true reds, and there are no true blues in this bunch.

Leaves and Stems

For the blocks, you'll need three or four greens from light to dark. Buy a half-yard of each, but if you decide to do an Appliqué Vine border, you're going to need extra. See page 81.

Supplies

Sewing Machine

You must have a machine that has a variable zigzag, which can be adjusted narrower or wider, as well as longer or shorter. You want to adjust your machine to make narrow stitches, very close together. The best stitch for this is the blind hemstitch which makes a pattern of two or three straight stitches and one "jump" stitch. Use your open toe appliqué foot with a quarter inch plate on either side, rather than the regular presser foot. It helps to have an extra bright light focused on your needle.

Thread

We use cotton machine embroidery thread in both the bobbin and the needle. DMC and Mettler sell a variety of colors. Some techniques use nylon thread, but we prefer the #50 machine embroidery thread as it is almost invisible if you match the color to the appliqué pieces. Prepare the bobbins by winding a few half full of different shades. Remember, the thread doesn't match the background; it matches the appliqué pieces. Look for blender colors, such as a gray green that can go with several different flowers.

Other supplies:

A paper marker

Pencil or Stanford's Sharpie ultra-fine point permanent marker.

2 kinds of glue

Water soluble glue stick (Kinko's, UHU, Carter's), Roxanne's Glue Baste It or Elmer's School Glue.

Scissors

Paper scissors, fabric scissors and a little sharp snipper scissors

A sharp pointed seam ripper
(NO you won't be ripping!)

Reynold's Freezer Paper
(available at the grocery store)

An iron and board

A surface to glue on, such as a plastic placemat

Appliqué Preparation

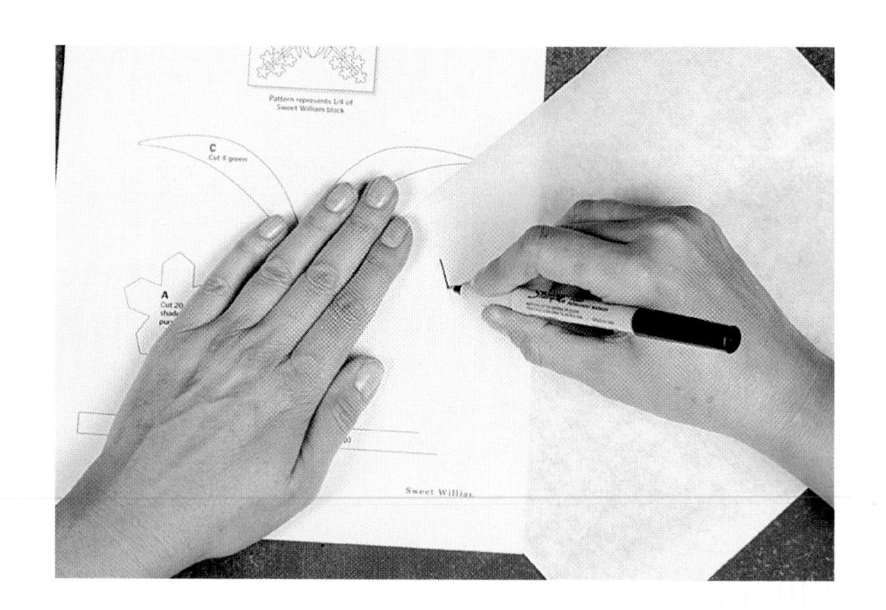

1. Trace the pattern templates onto the dull side of the freezer paper. Do not add seam allowances. (Most of the patterns in the series are reversible, but a few, such as the leaves in the Dandelion, page 30, have a directionality.) Remember to flip these pattern pieces for the reversible units or they will be going the wrong direction.

2. Cut out your shapes right on the line. Accuracy in cutting at this stage really pays off later. (If you want to cut four shapes at once, just trace the first one on one sheet of freezer paper. Cut three more sheets of freezer paper. Place the sheet with the drawing on the top and layer them with the shiny side down. With a hot iron fuse the four sheets together around the edges and make little taps in the center of each pattern piece. Then cut out four pieces at a time. Separate the shapes. If they tear or are fused permanently you've used too much heat. Try it again by just making fast swipes with the iron.)

3. Press the freezer paper shapes with the shiny side down to the wrong side of the fabrics. Leave a space between the pieces so you can add a 3/16" seam allowance when you cut out the fabric.

4. Cut out the paper backed shapes, adding your 3/16" seam allowance as you cut. (We feel that the usual 1/4" seam allowance is too big. On some very small or very curvy pieces—this pattern doesn't have any—you may want to use an even smaller seam allowance.)

5. Clip the inside curves on pattern pieces. (Many of the flower shapes, such as the Wild Rose, the Sweet William or the Morning Glory, have inside curves or "v" cuts. Clip the inside curves as shown, cutting right down to, but not into the paper. You don't need to trim outside curves.)

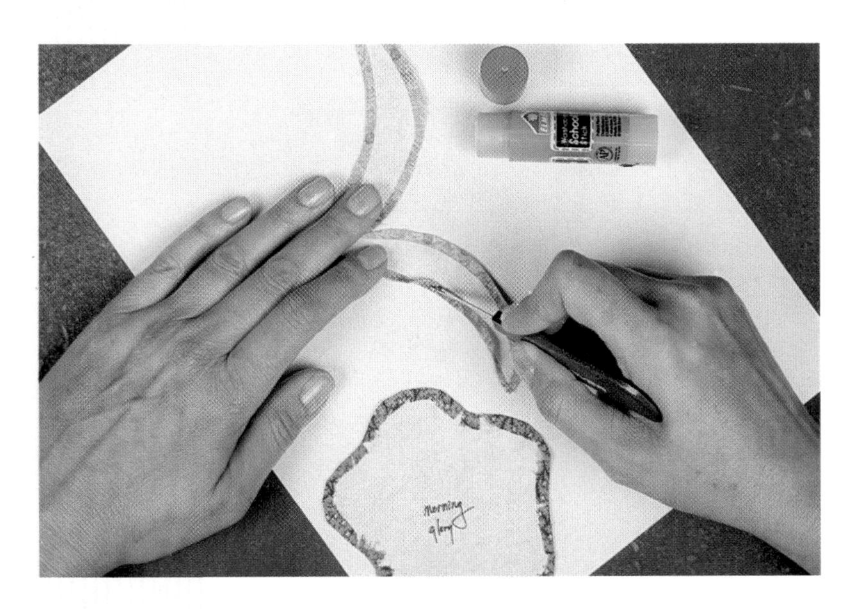

6. Fold and glue the seam allowance to the dull side of the freezer paper with your glue stick. Again, accuracy in this step really pays off in the final look. (You can use the point of a seam ripper to manipulate the fabric over the paper as you glue. Ease any ripples that appear in the seam allowances by flattening them out. Glue down any threads that want to wiggle out in the "v" cuts.)

7. Position the shapes onto the background fabric. (You can pin the shapes where they belong, but we like to use a water soluble white glue, such as Roxanne's Glue Baste It with its accurate applicator. We use a lot of glue at this step, making little dots right around the edge of each piece.)

Sewing

1. Prepare your machine to sew a short, narrow version of the blind hemstitch. Other stitches that will work are overcast or zig-zag stitches.

2. Load the machine with thread to match the appliqué pieces. (Changing the thread to match each piece gets to be a little tiresome, so I usually prepare several blocks at once and then sew all my green leaves and stems at the same time. Then I change to yellow and do all the yellow pieces in all the blocks.)

3. Set your work on the machine so that the stitch is in the ditch right next to the appliqué shape and sew around each shape. The hem stitch will make two straight stitches in the background of the fabric and then the jump stitch will catch the appliqué. The fine thread hardly shows in the background since it is right on the edge of the appliqué, and the jump stitch hardly shows because it is the same color as the appliqué. The real skill in sewing is to make sure that jump stitch goes into the appliqué every time. You'll learn to control the feed and the placement of the jump stitches with practice.

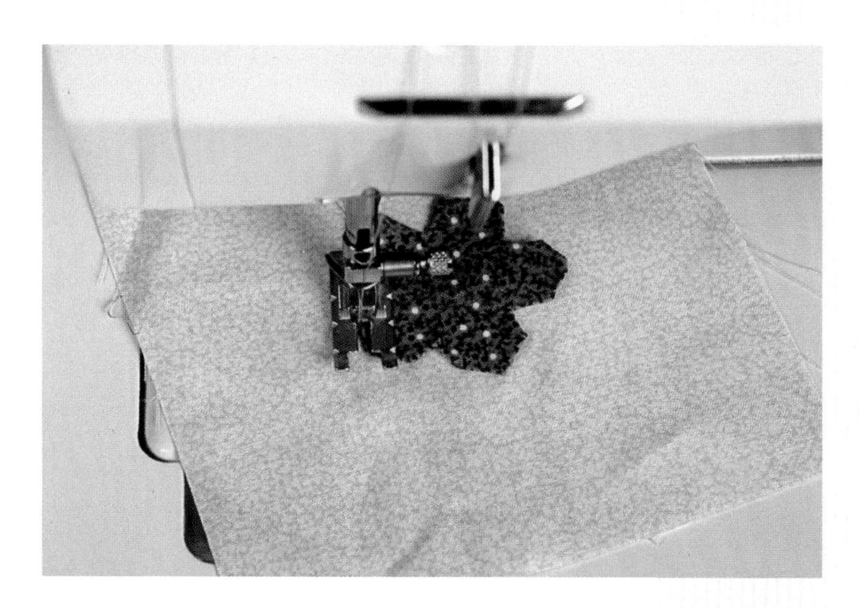

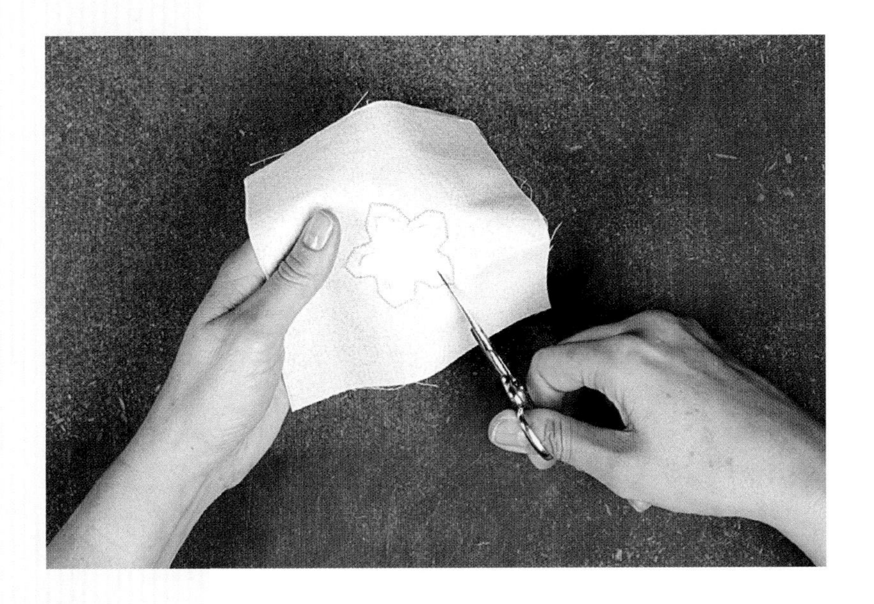

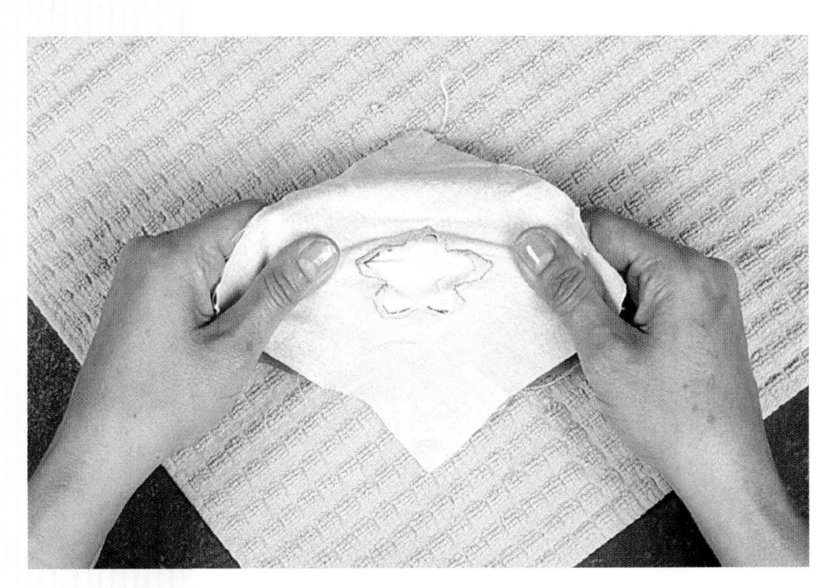

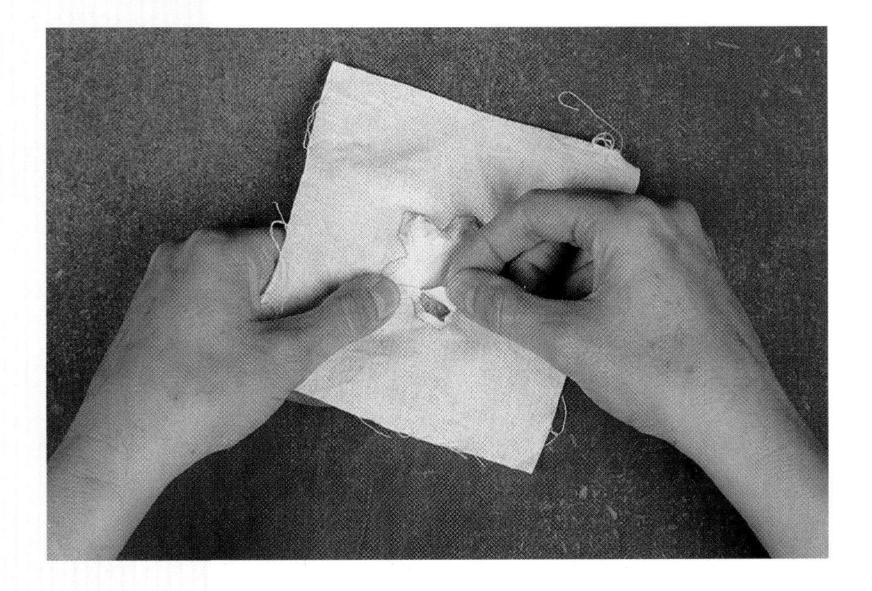

Removing the Freezer Paper

1. When you are finished with the block, cut out the background behind each appliqué shape leaving about 1/4" allowance.

2. Soak the block in cool water for 60 seconds. Roll the wet block in a towel for five minutes so the freezer paper really absorbs the water.

3. Lay the block flat and tug it diagonally in both directions, freeing the freezer paper from the glue and the stitches.

4. Remove all the freezer paper. The freezer paper should come out in large pieces. If you feel you have to use tweezers rather than your fingers, you need to go back a few steps and soak the block again.

5. Dry the block in a cool dryer with a towel (preferably a white towel – and preferably a towel you just use for drying fabric). Do not iron the block until it is dry. Heat and steam can aggravate bleeding.

6. Press your dry block, and admire your work.

The Appliqué Blocks

MASSACHUSETTS born and bred, Sara Tappan Doolittle Robinson was charmed by the landscape she found upon setting her well-shod foot on the rich, black soil of Kansas and western Missouri in March 1855.

"The face of this country is beautiful beyond all comparison," wrote the young wife in her diary. She saw prairie grass as tall as a person's head while seated in a carriage, and flowering shrubs that reminded her of "dear New England homes, where art and taste have labored long."

In these pages, quiltmakers can make the acquaintance of pioneer women like Sara one stitch at a time. The flora that greeted Sara, Laura Ingalls Wilder and other women who came here to sow new lives has inspired a new series of *Kansas City Star* quilt patterns called "Prairie Flower" – the first designed for *The Star* in 40 years. The first *Star* quilt patterns were published between 1928 and 1961 as routine features in this newspaper and sister publications.

Bittersweet

American Bittersweet, *Celastraccae scandens*

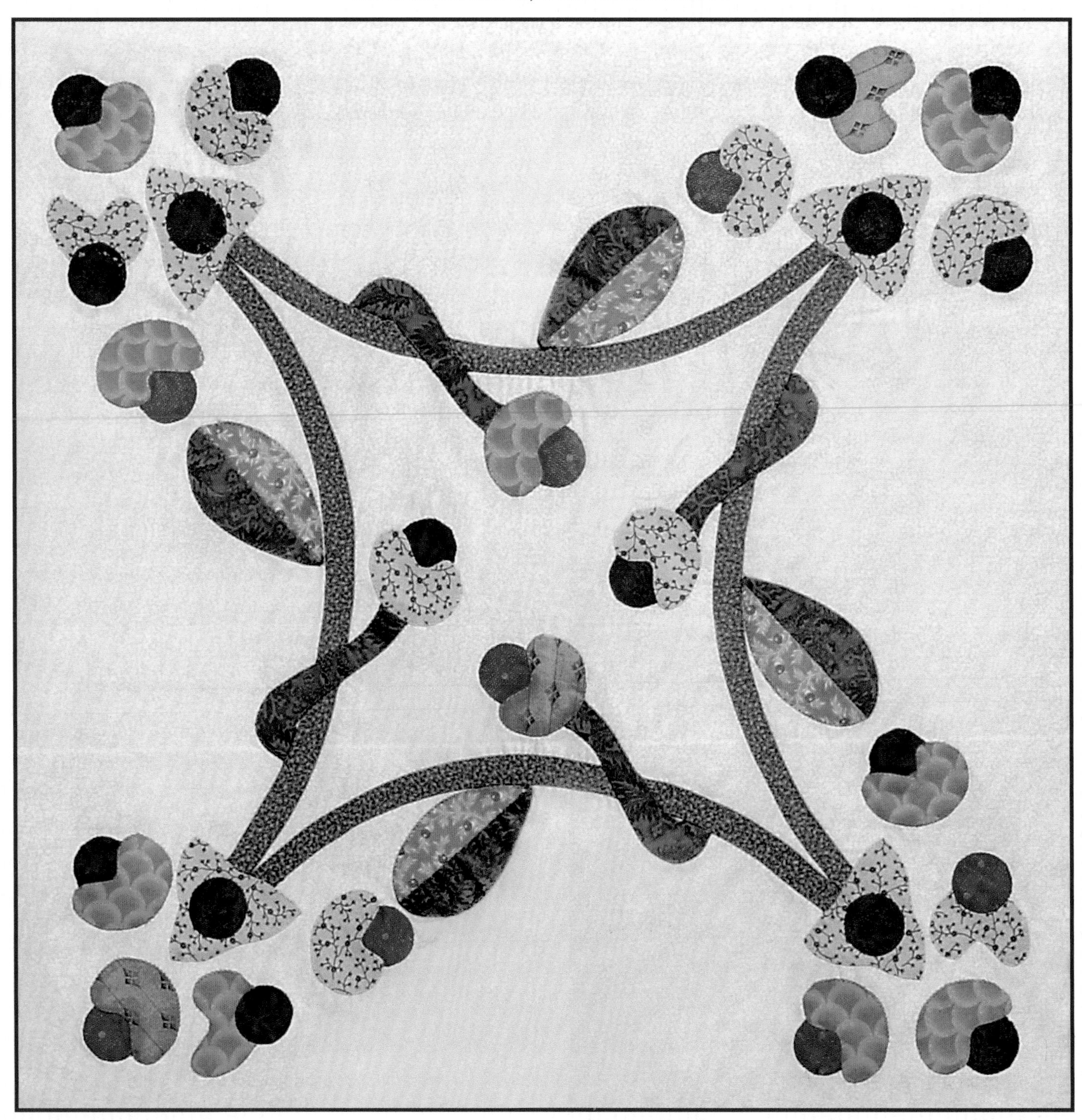

BITTERSWEET – block #1,
Blocks 1-12, machine appliquéd by Jean Stanclift, Lawrence, Kan., 2001

THE WAY SHE FOUND IT...

"April 13th, 1855. We wrote, read and walked out into the woods, or took a long walk upon the prairie. The woods near here were full of gooseberries and grape vines. Bitter-sweet and running roses wound their tendrils upon the branches, and climbed high among the trees. The red berries of the bitter-sweet were still hanging on the vines."

"April 17th. We leave for Lawrence this morning. I have just been into the woods, after some rose and gooseberry bushes, not knowing whether I can get them near Lawrence." —SARA T.D. ROBINSON

Sara T.D. Robinson with the Shawnee Mission behind her.

SARA T. D. ROBINSON came to the Great Plains in the spring of 1855, when she was 27 years old. Her husband, Charles, had come earlier as an agent of a New England anti-slavery group to found a free-state colony in the Kansas Territory. While waiting for the builders to finish her house in Lawrence atop Mount Oread, she stayed at the Shawnee Baptist Mission. Like many women arriving in a new landscape, she looked for reminders of her old home among the wild flowers.

Sara probably found the native American Bittersweet, which is rare now, replaced by the similar Oriental Bittersweet.

Sara Robinson's diary was first published in 1856 as *Kansas: Its Interior & Exterior Life*. She wrote it as a political plea for the free-state cause and the book went through many editions. It's out of print but you may be able to find one in a library or used-book source.

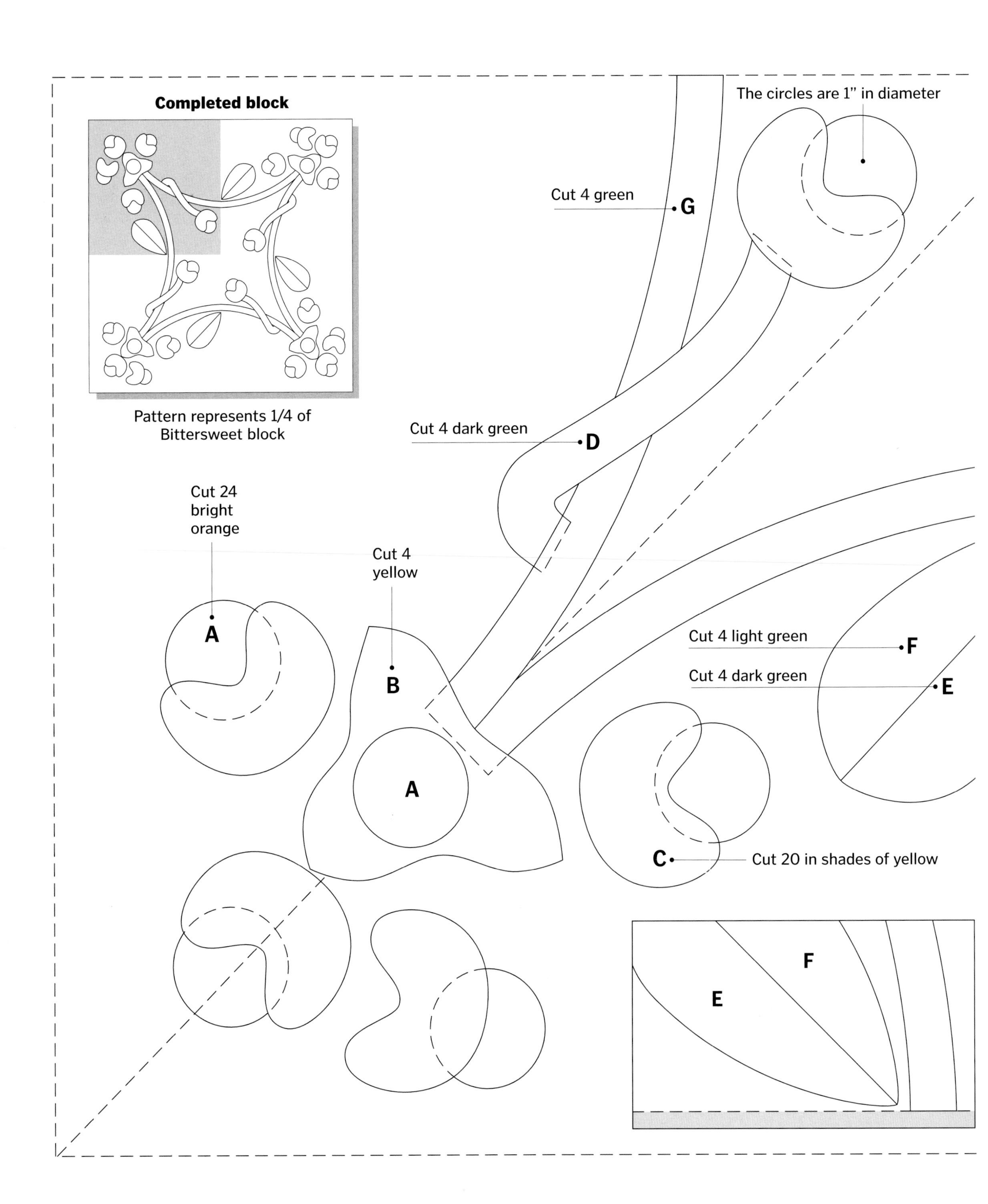
Completed block
Pattern represents 1/4 of Bittersweet block
The circles are 1" in diameter
Cut 4 green
G
Cut 4 dark green
D
Cut 24 bright orange
A
Cut 4 yellow
B
A
Cut 4 light green
F
Cut 4 dark green
E
C
Cut 20 in shades of yellow
F
E

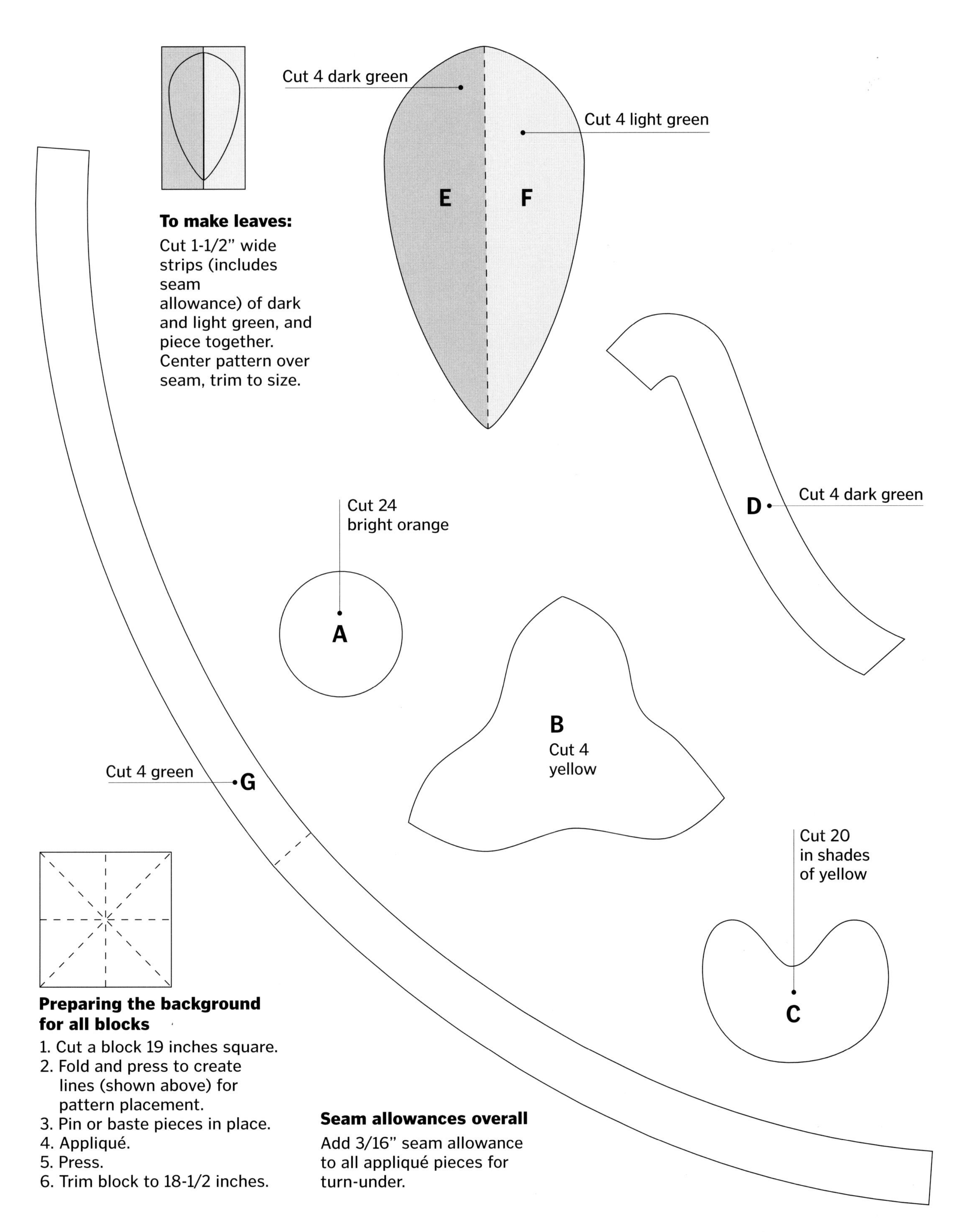
Cut 4 dark green
Cut 4 light green
E
F
To make leaves:
Cut 1-1/2" wide strips (includes seam allowance) of dark and light green, and piece together. Center pattern over seam, trim to size.
Cut 4 dark green
D
Cut 24 bright orange
A
B
Cut 4 yellow
Cut 4 green
G
Cut 20 in shades of yellow
C
Preparing the background for all blocks
1. Cut a block 19 inches square.
2. Fold and press to create lines (shown above) for pattern placement.
3. Pin or baste pieces in place.
4. Appliqué.
5. Press.
6. Trim block to 18-1/2 inches.
Seam allowances overall
Add 3/16" seam allowance to all appliqué pieces for turn-under.

Dandelion

Cat's Ear Dandelion, *Hypochoeris radicala*

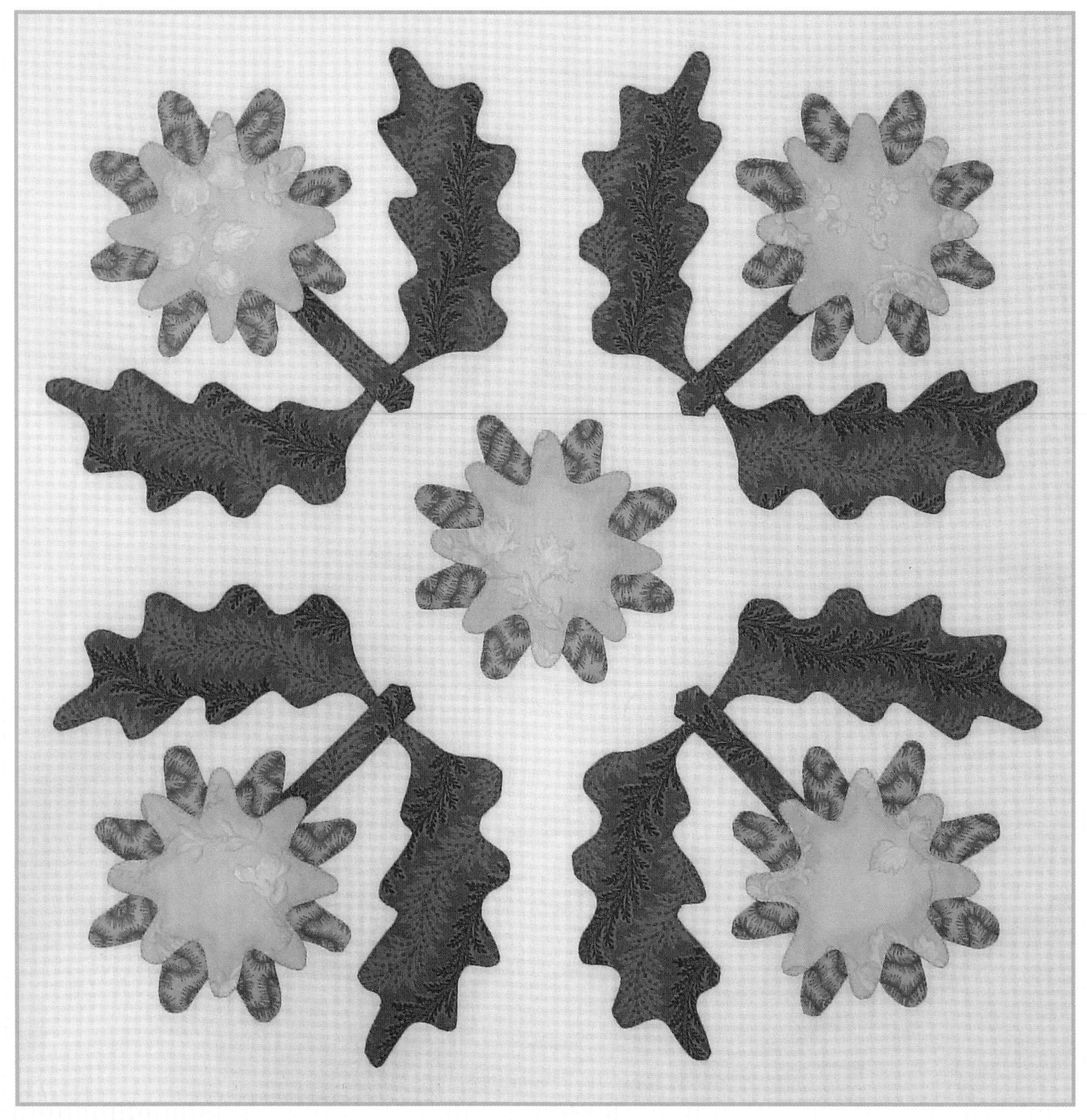

DANDELION – block #2

THE WAY SHE FOUND IT...

"I WISH YOU could see the grass here, it is as high in the Park as it is when papa turns out the cows. I have seen some small dandy lions and the trees are nearly ready to open...I send a little scrap of what is here called cedar. They plant them in their yards. They say they are like ours but I know better. You notice if it is. Crush it and notice how peculiar it smells."

—SUSAN (ELSIE) CURRIER

CEDAR TREES are one of the few evergreens that thrive on the plains. Unknown woman and grandchild. About 1915.

SUSAN (ELSIE) CURRIER came to Junction City, Kan., to marry Leslie Snow, who was stationed here as a pension examiner. Her chatty letters to her mother back home in New Hampshire were an invitation to join in her adventure in the West. On March 20, 1889, she gave Mamma the above glimpse of early spring on the prairie.

There are so many kinds of dandelions; yet their subtlety is usually wasted on us. We rarely see them as anything but weeds. The Cat's Ear in the block has a rounded serration on the leaves.

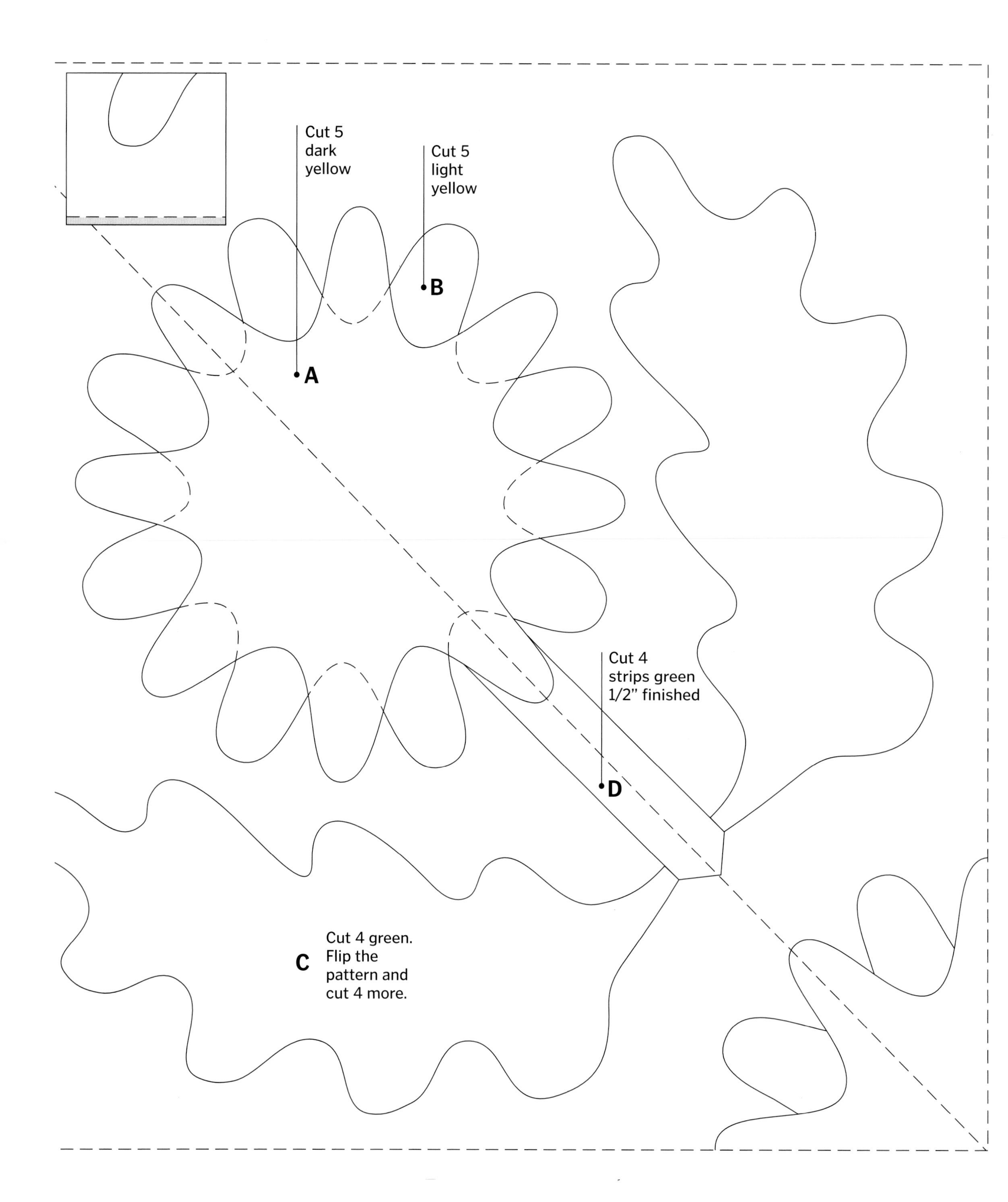
Cut 5
dark
yellow
Cut 5
light
yellow
B
A
Cut 4
strips green
1/2" finished
D
C
Cut 4 green.
Flip the
pattern and
cut 4 more.

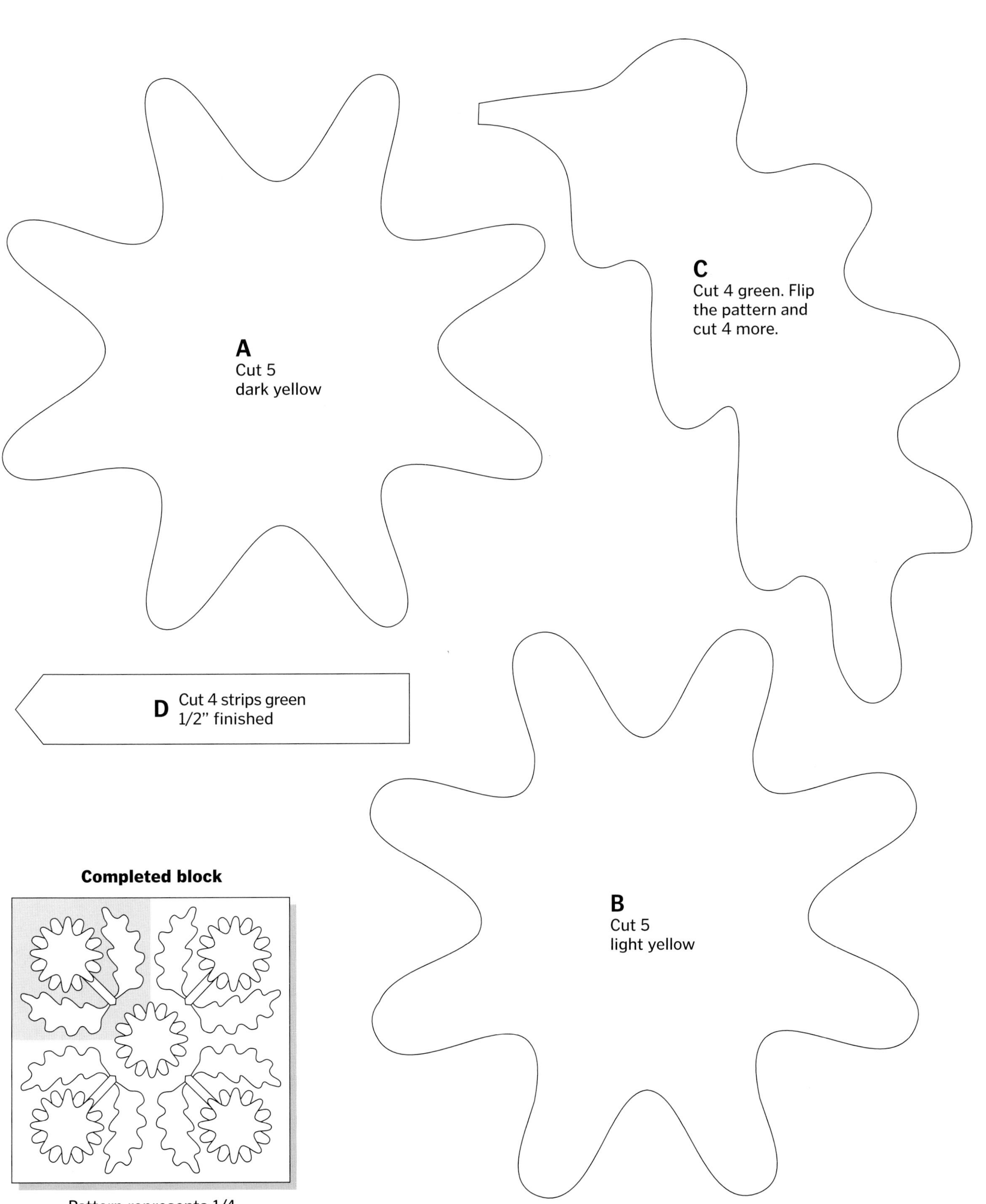

Pattern represents 1/4
of Dandelion block

Wood Sorrel

Violet Wood Sorrel, *Oxalis violacea*

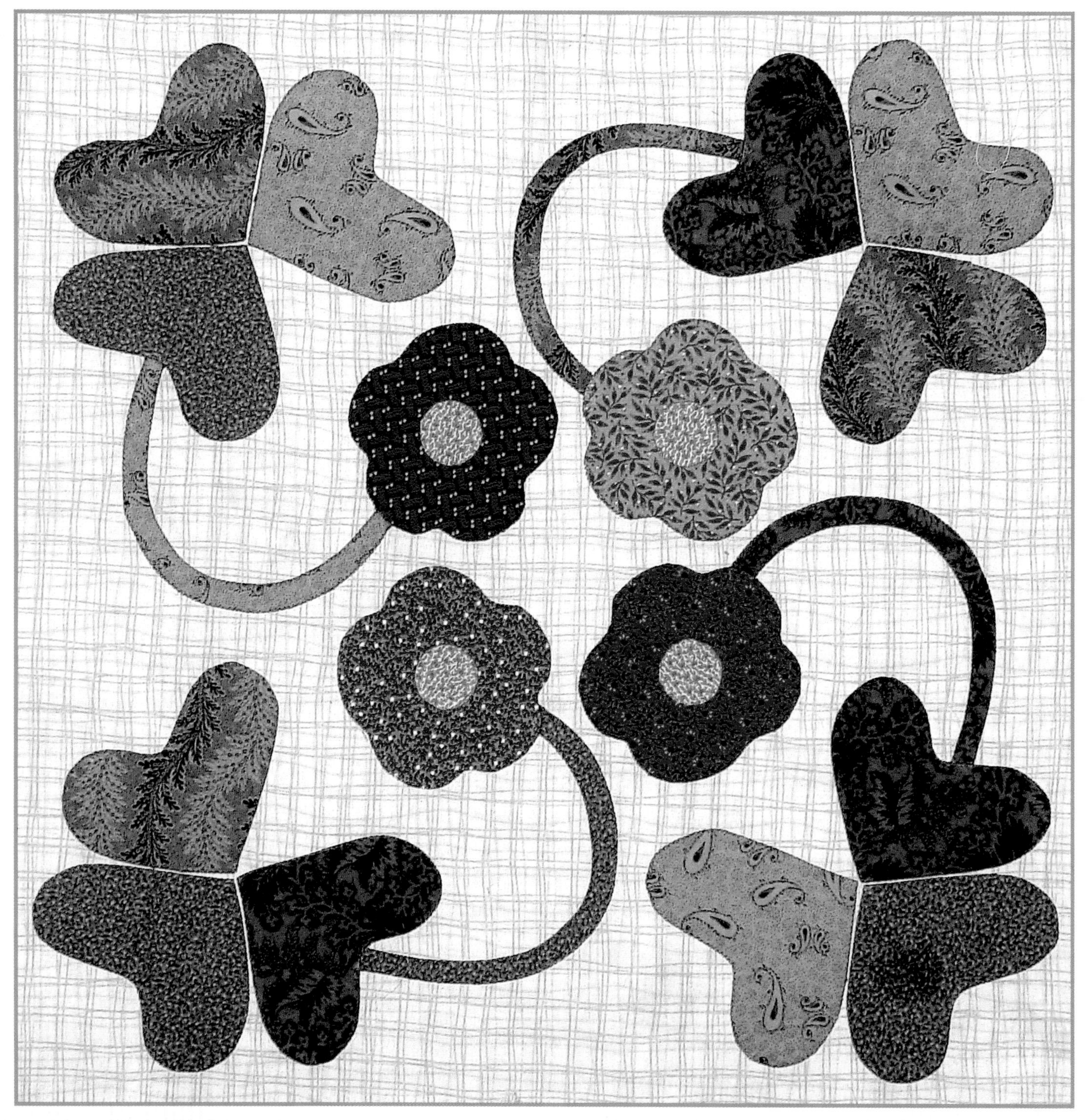

Wood Sorrel – block #3

THE WAY SHE FOUND IT...

"MAY 7, 1871. Several of us started out for the bluff. Two miles and a half. We found eleven new kinds of flowers. The prairie was covered with them. We went to the top and found verbenas, geraniums, celery, sorrel and pennyroyal."

—LUNA WARNER

Luna Warner as a young woman

LUNA WARNER was a 16-year-old pioneer whose diary kept good account of her interest in wildflowers and quiltmaking. She liked to count the varieties of flowers on the prairie near Downs, Kan. By June 8th, she'd seen 71 different types.

She also documented her patchwork. "July 9. I have 22 squares of an album bed quilt done."

This third square of your sampler quilt is the wood sorrel, a small oxalis or shamrock. Sarah Everett, living in Osawatomie in 1856, described it in a letter to a friend as "a little flower peculiarly beautiful.... I never noticed it till I saw it on the prairies in Kansas although the leaves are perfectly familiar. The flower is a fine purplish pink and altogether quite enchanting."

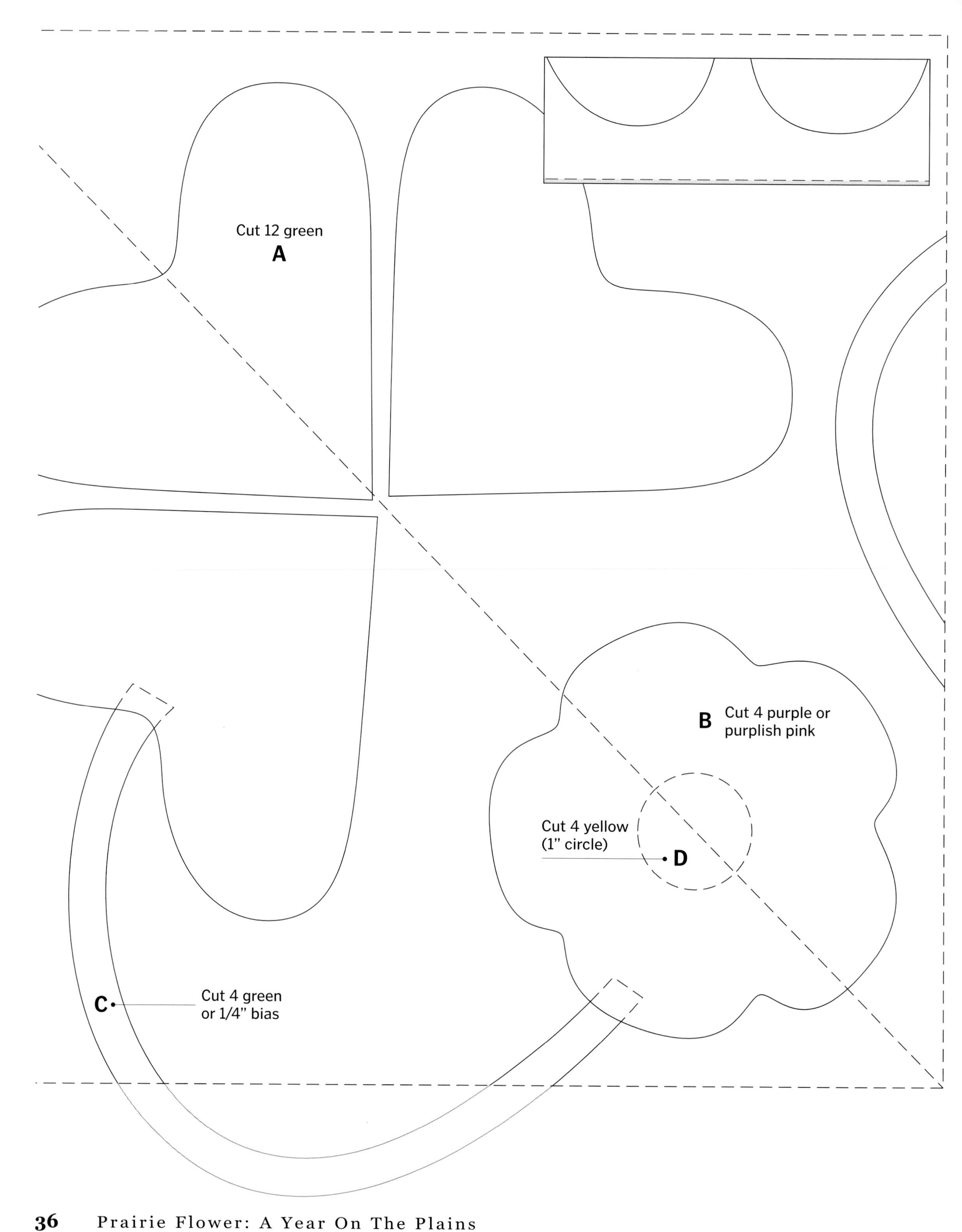
Cut 12 green
A
B
Cut 4 purple or
purplish pink
Cut 4 yellow
(1" circle)
D
C
Cut 4 green
or 1/4" bias

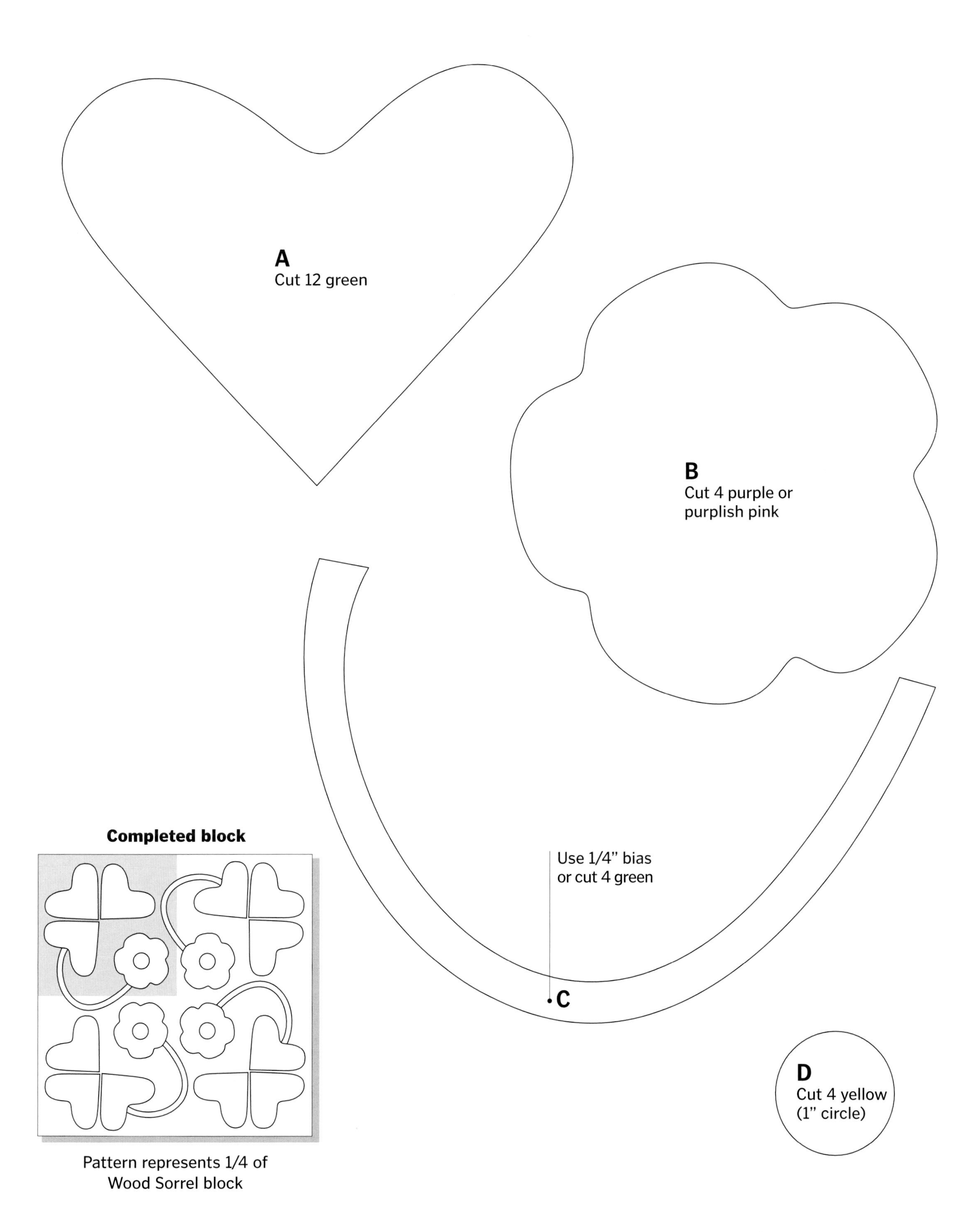

Pattern represents 1/4 of
Wood Sorrel block

Sweet William

Phlox maculata

Sweet William – block #4

The Way She Found It...

"He never brings me cultivated flowers but always the wild blossoms of field and woodland and I think them much more beautiful." —Laura Ingalls Wilder

Laura Ingalls Wilder

Wilder home in Missouri

Laura Ingalls Wilder lived in many places, from the big woods in Minnesota to the southern Kansas prairie. She spent most of her life near Mansfield, Mo., where she wrote her Little House series. Laura loved wildflowers and named her only daughter Rose after a favorite.

Long before she began her books about growing up in a pioneering family, Laura wrote articles for the *Missouri Ruralist* magazine. In 1917, her husband Almanzo presented her with a bouquet of wild flowers including Sweet Williams, a wild phlox.

The Sweet Williams reminded her of her schooldays when "someone discovered that the blossoms could be pulled from the stem and, by wetting their faces, could be stuck to the pieces of glass in whatever fashion they were arranged. They dried on the glass and would stay that way for hours and, looked at thru the glass, were very pretty."

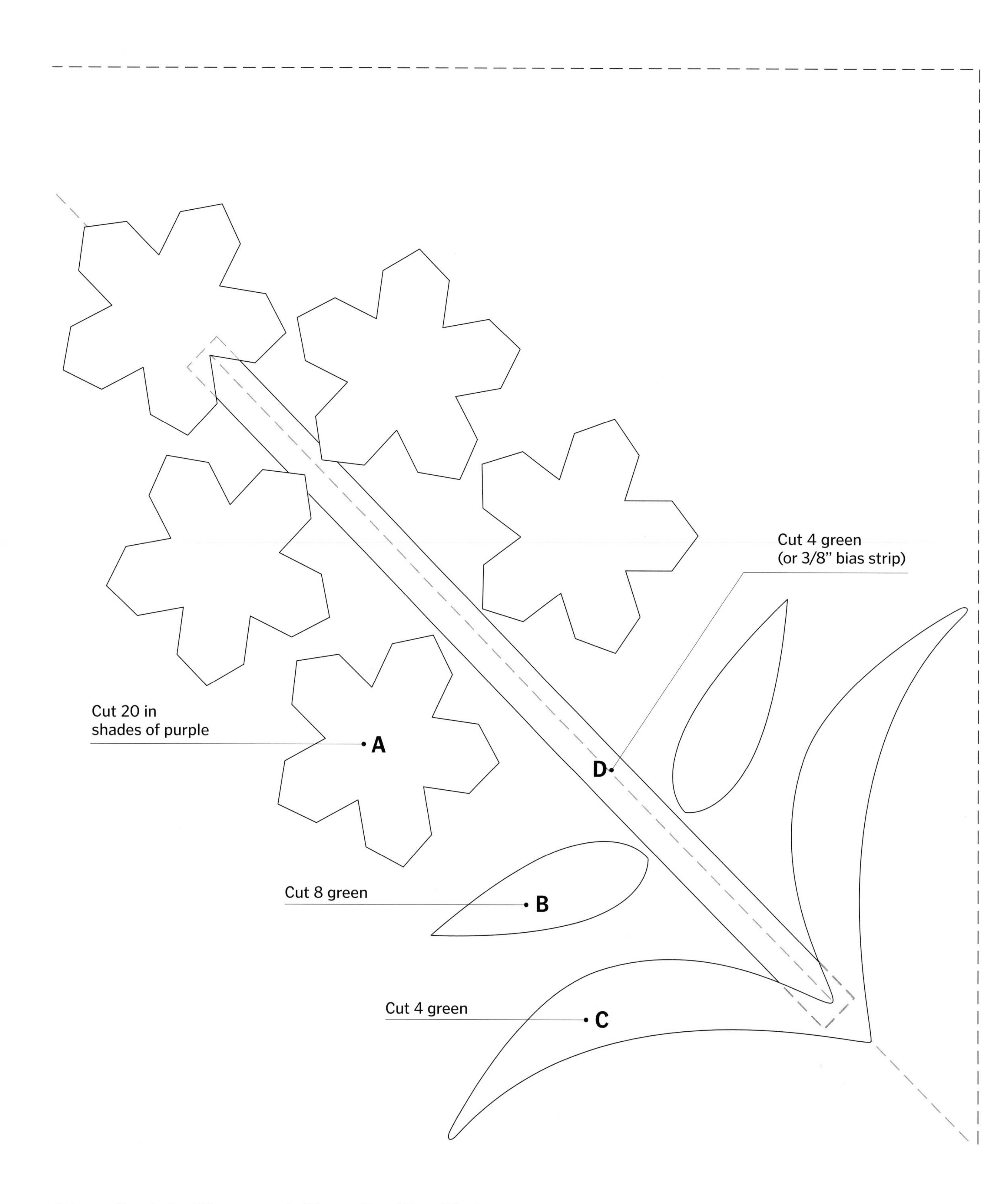
Cut 4 green
(or 3/8" bias strip)
Cut 20 in
shades of purple
A
D
Cut 8 green
B
Cut 4 green
C

Completed block

Pattern represents 1/4 of Sweet William block

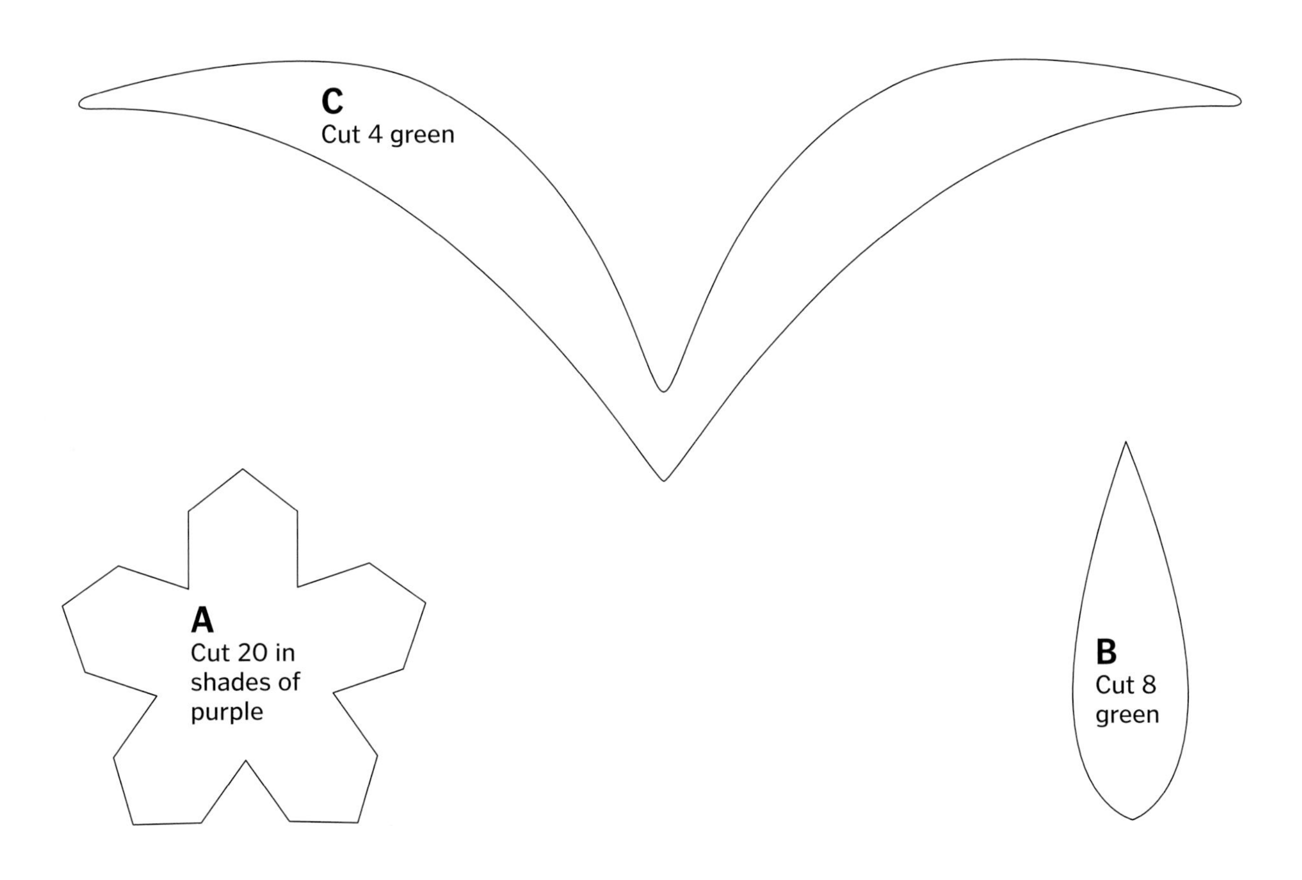

D Cut 4 green (or 3/8" bias strip)

Wild Rose

Pasture Rose, *Rosa Carolina*

WILD ROSE – block #5

THE WAY SHE FOUND IT...

"PASSED ONE LONE TREE, which was cedar, looks verry singular there being no tree or shrub for a hundred miles. . . scenery delightful, find some of the most beautiful flowers none that we see in the states except wild roses, I love to walk along and gather them." —AMELIA HAMMOND HADLEY

IS THIS UNKNOWN couple celebrating their wedding or an anniversary? Many young pioneer couples spent their honeymoon on the overland trail. About 1920.

AMELIA HAMMOND HADLEY married in April, 1851, in Galesburg, Ill., and four days later began a wagon trip to Oregon over the Platte River trail. A honeymoon in May may be the best time to view the prairies. On May 30, in what is now Nebraska, she wrote in her diary of traveling alongside the river.

The Pasture Rose or the Carolina Rose grows all over the country. The low shrubs with their pink flowers are an especially welcome sight as the temperature rises in late spring on the prairie.

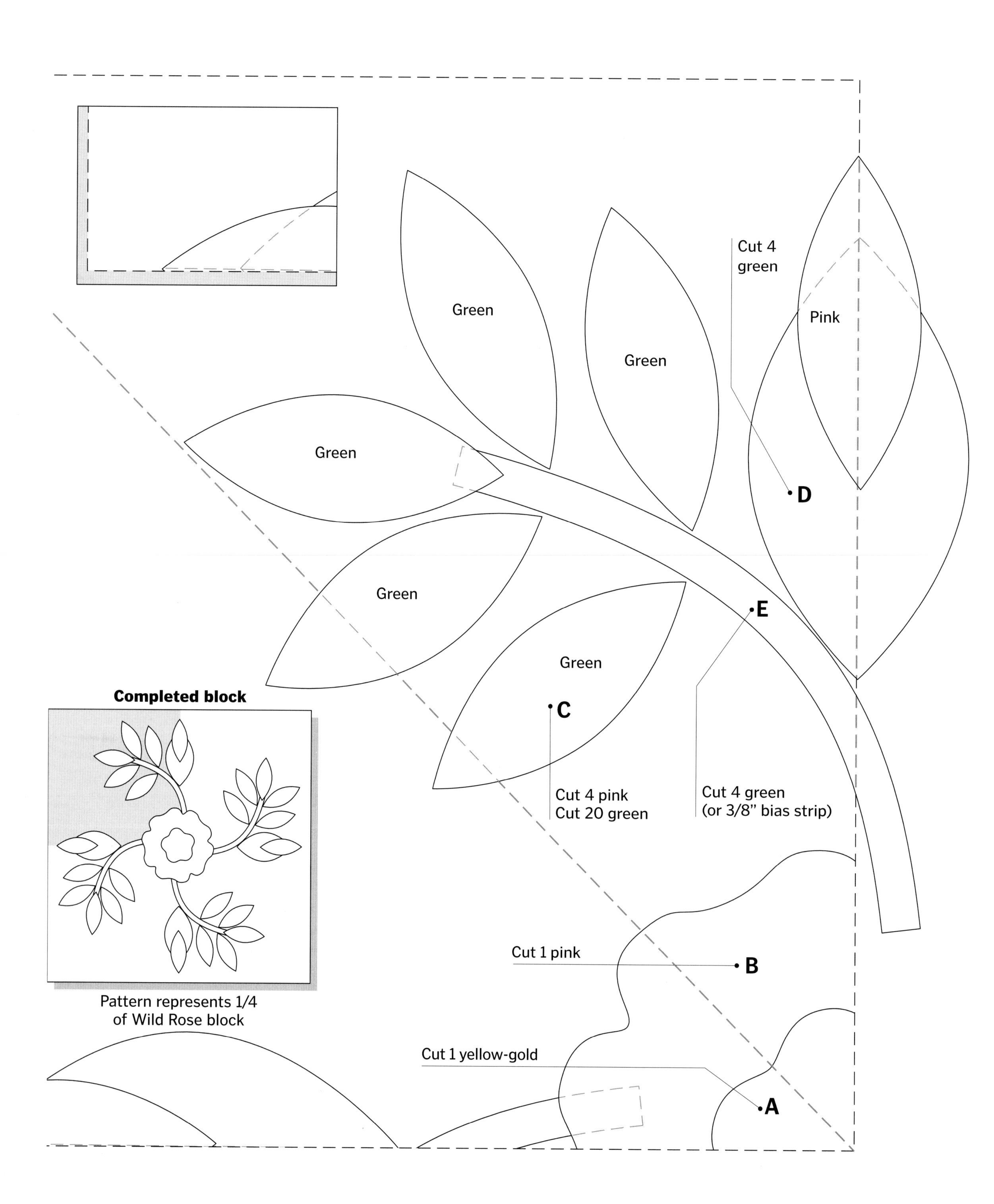
Green
Green
Cut 4
green
Pink
Green
D
Green
E
Green
Green
C
Completed block
Cut 4 pink
Cut 20 green
Cut 4 green
(or 3/8" bias strip)
Cut 1 pink
B
Pattern represents 1/4
of Wild Rose block
Cut 1 yellow-gold
A

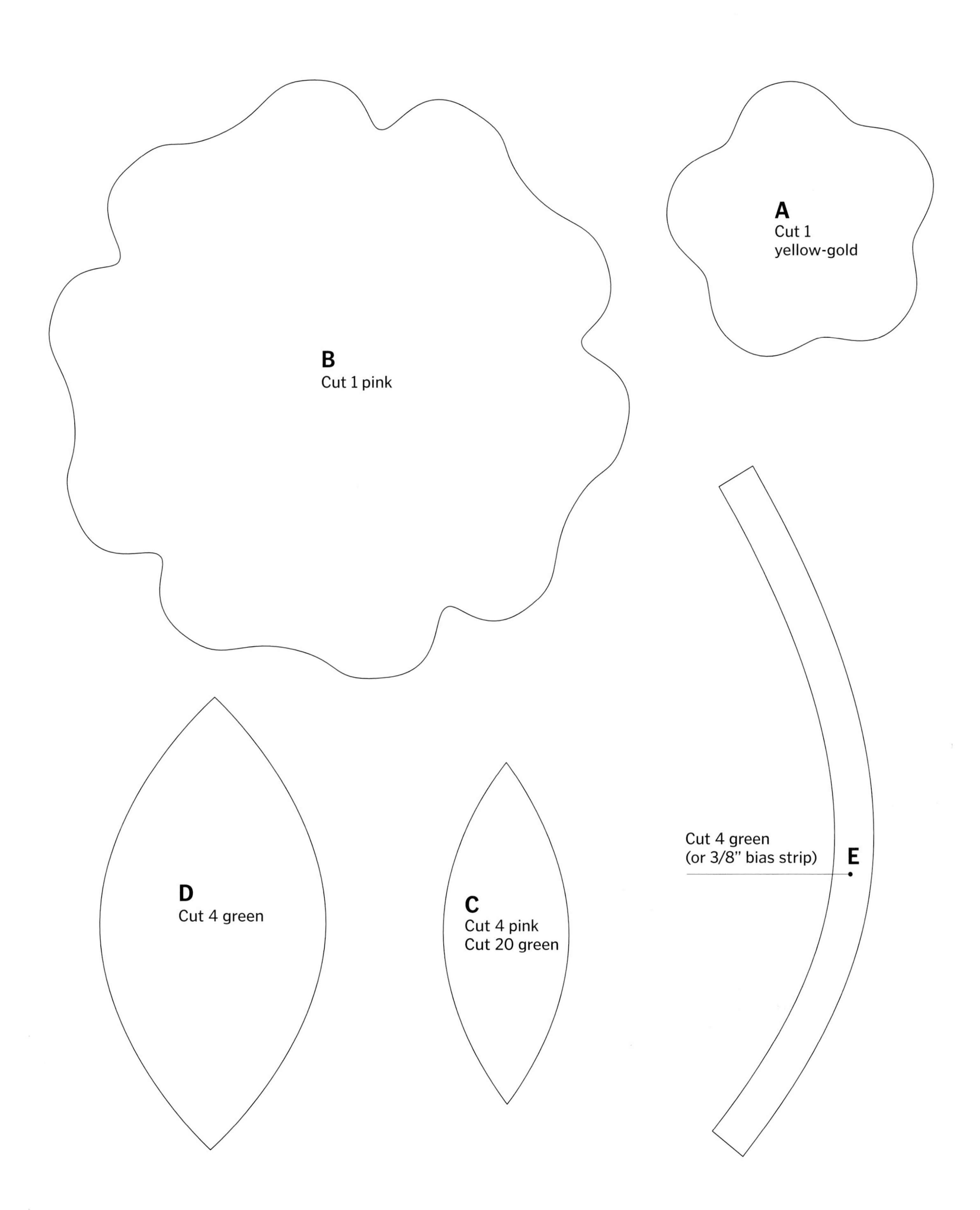
A
Cut 1
yellow-gold
B
Cut 1 pink
Cut 4 green
(or 3/8" bias strip)
E
D
Cut 4 green
C
Cut 4 pink
Cut 20 green

Wild Cucumber

Bur Cucumber, *Sicyos angulatus*

WILD CUCUMBER – block #6

THE WAY SHE FOUND IT...

"THE LEAF AND FLOWER I enclose is what they call here the wild cucumber. We all have it trained up at our porches, and it makes a beautiful shade." —CAROLINE FREY WINNE

OVER TIME, settlers learned to transplant native plants to their gardens. About 1925.

CAROLINE FREY WINNE was an Army wife stationed at Sidney on the edge of the Great Plains in far western Nebraska. Like many newcomers she was uncomfortable living in the treeless prairies. In letters to an Eastern friend in spring, 1875, she wrote, "I envy you your beautiful flowers, and still more will envy you for your trees in summer and spring...I wish I had taken more lessons of Della in flower culture. We are going to try to have some flowers here this summer, but I don't expect to succeed. Only hearty things will grow here." By August, she had figured out what was hardy, transplanting native plants to her yard.

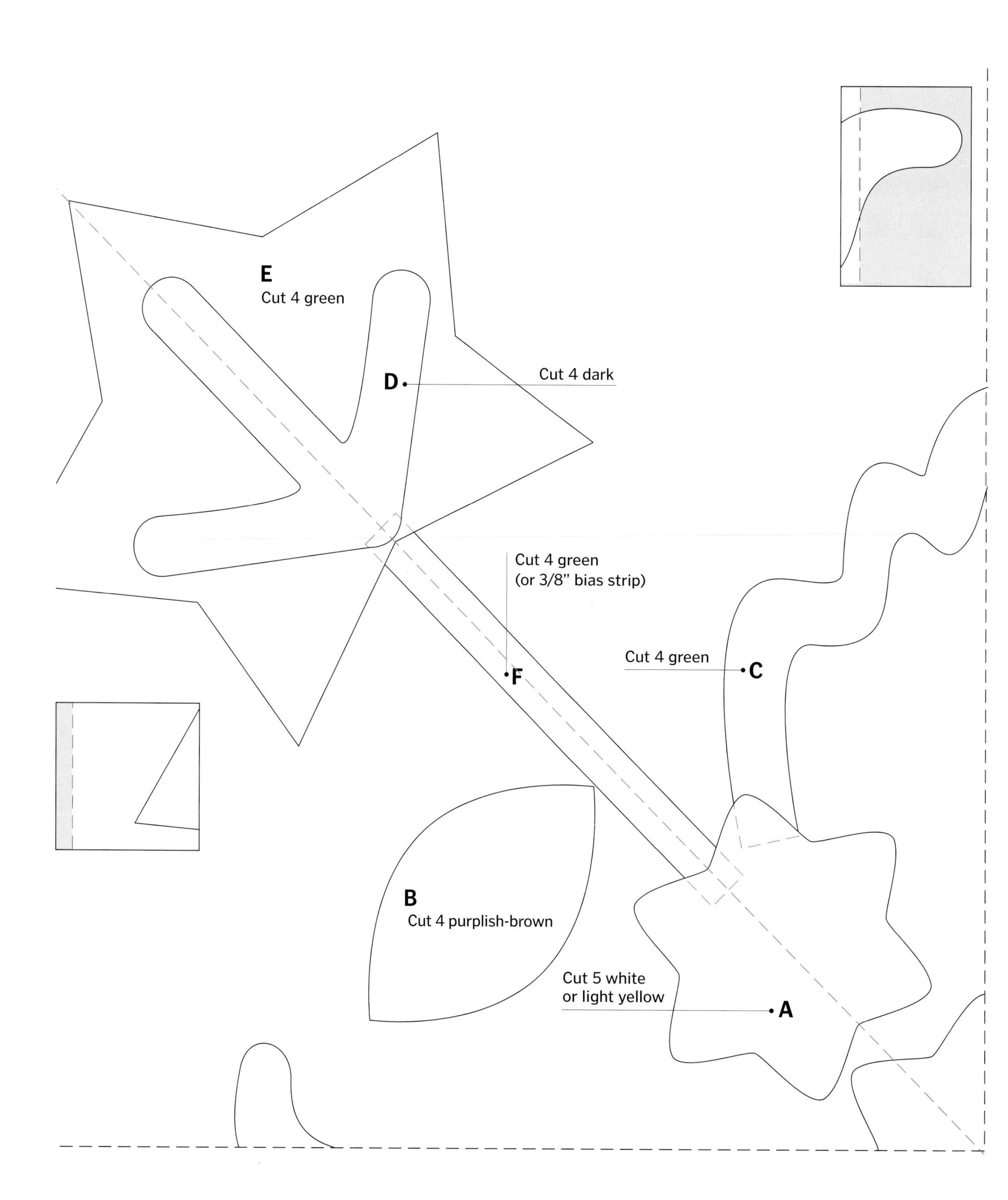
E
Cut 4 green
D
Cut 4 dark
Cut 4 green
(or 3/8" bias strip)
F
Cut 4 green
C
B
Cut 4 purplish-brown
Cut 5 white
or light yellow
A

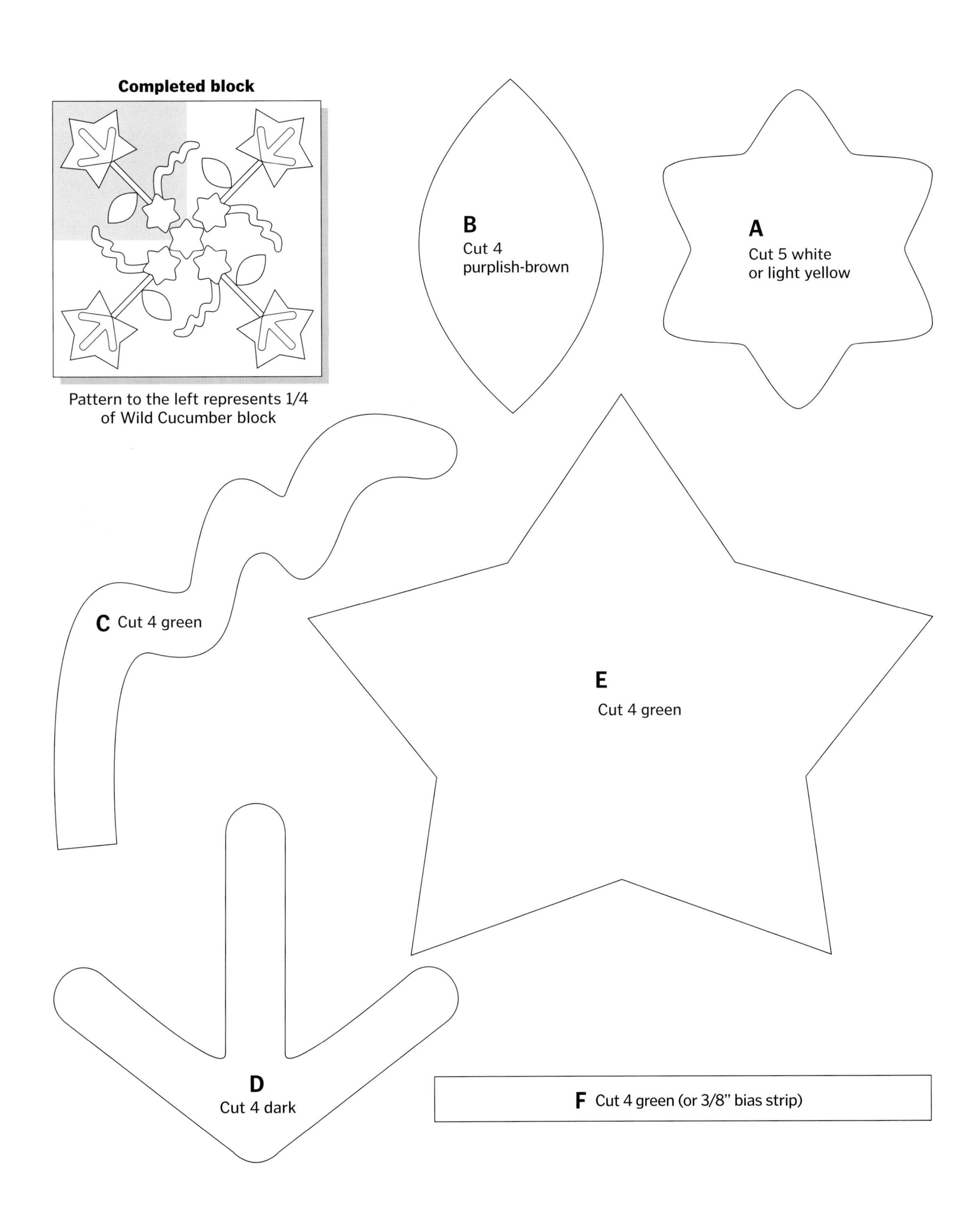
Completed block
Pattern to the left represents 1/4
of Wild Cucumber block
B
Cut 4
purplish-brown
A
Cut 5 white
or light yellow
C Cut 4 green
E
Cut 4 green
D
Cut 4 dark
F Cut 4 green (or 3/8" bias strip)

Missouri Primrose

Oenothera missouriensis

MISSOURI PRIMROSE – block #7

The way she found it...

"June 16, 1846. I never could have believed we could have travelled so far with so little difficulty. The prairie between the Blue and Platte rivers is abundant beyond description. Never have I seen so varied a country....We have found the wild tulip, the primrose, the lupine, the ear-drop, the larkspur, and creeping holyhock, and a beautfiul flower resembling the bloom of the beach tree, but in bunches as big as a small sugar-leaf, and of every variety of shade to red and green. I botanize and read some, but cook a 'heap' more." —Tamsen Donner

Decades after their trip west these unknown couples pose with the old-fashioned yoke of oxen. About 1935.

Tamsen Donner was one of the first pioneers across the prairie, traveling with her family in 1846. Her name is familiar because she was one of the ill-fated Donner-Reed party, one who froze to death in the California mountains. A letter from her survives, describing the pleasant part of the trip after they left Independence, Mo.

The primrose that delighted Tamsen might have been the Missouri Primrose, a bright yellow flower that blooms in the evenings. Also called the Ozark Sundrop, the wild perennial is native to the area from Nebraska and Iowa south to Texas.

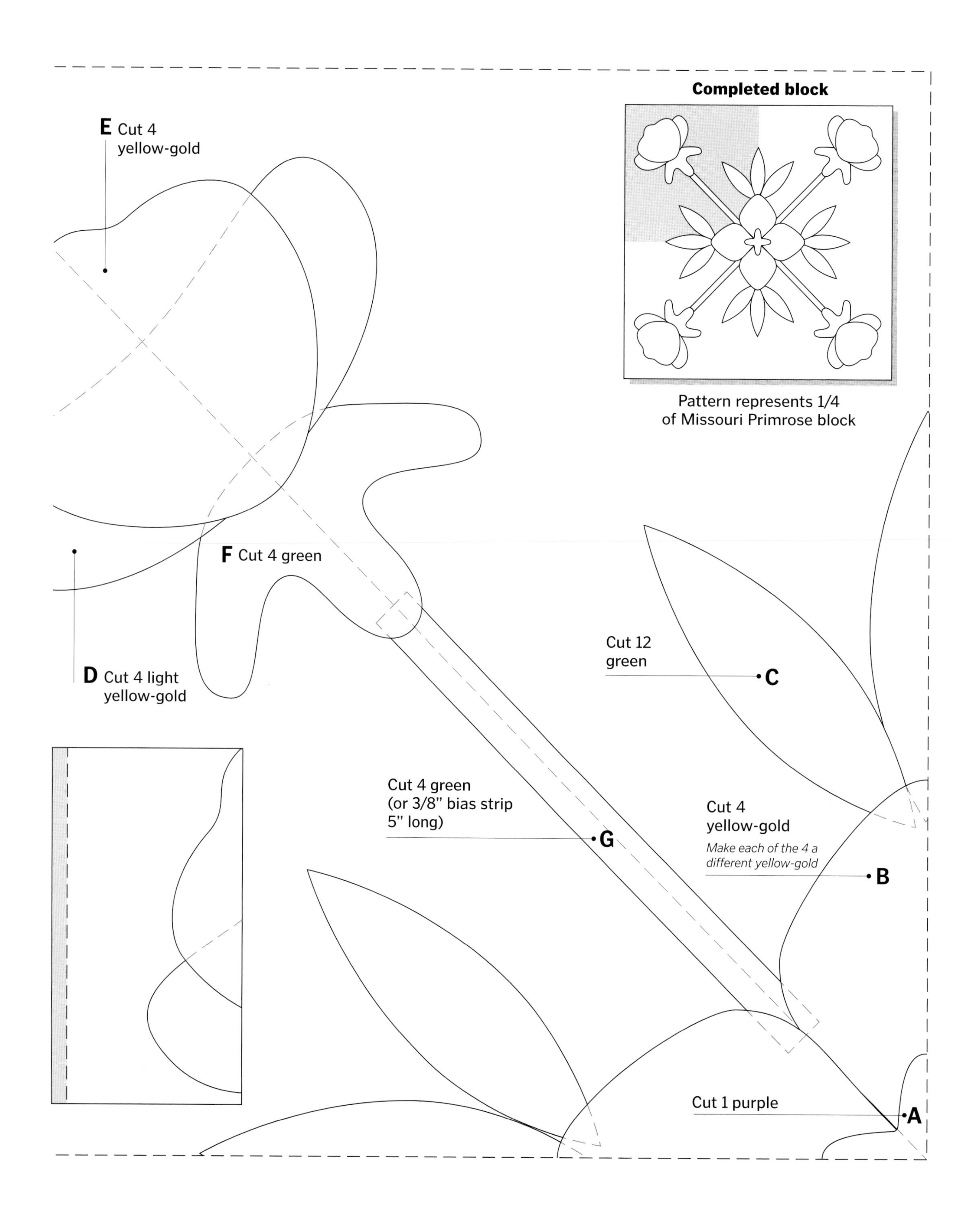

Completed block
Pattern represents 1/4
of Missouri Primrose block
E Cut 4
yellow-gold
F Cut 4 green
D Cut 4 light
yellow-gold
Cut 12
green
C
Cut 4 green
(or 3/8" bias strip
5" long)
G
Cut 4
yellow-gold
Make each of the 4 a
different yellow-gold
B
Cut 1 purple
A

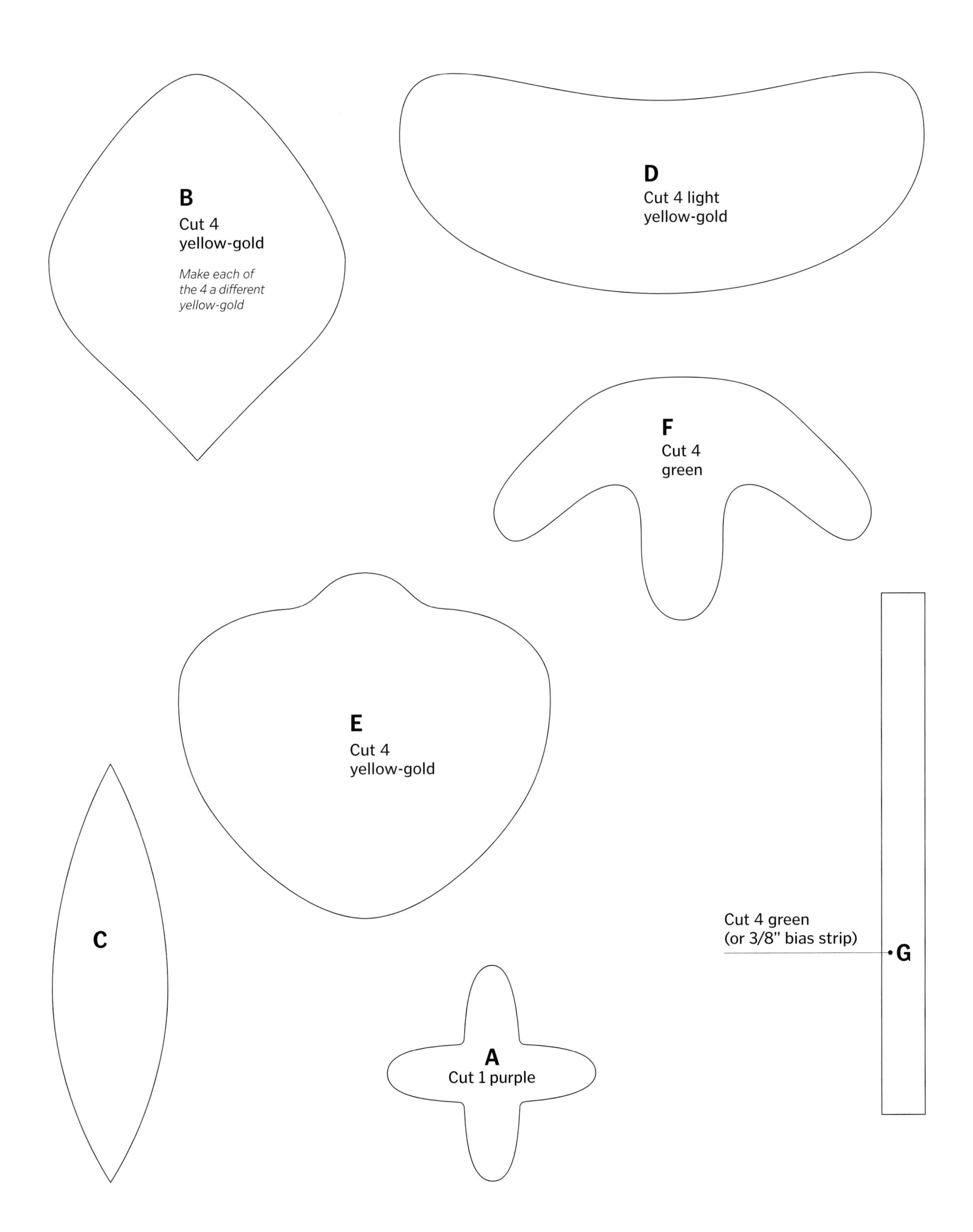
B
Cut 4
yellow-gold
Make each of
the 4 a different
yellow-gold
D
Cut 4 light
yellow-gold
F
Cut 4
green
E
Cut 4
yellow-gold
C
Cut 4 green
(or 3/8" bias strip)
G
A
Cut 1 purple

Wild Morning Glory

Hedge Bindweed, *Calystegia sepium*

Wild Morning Glory – block #7

THE WAY SHE FOUND IT...

"June 1, 1851. The Pararie is covered with beautiful little flowers whose fragrance surpassed any garden flowers. There is a modest little white flower which peeps up among the green grass which particularly strikes my fancy. I call it the Pararie Flower." —HARRIET TALCOTT BUCKINGHAM

HARRIET TALCOTT BUCKINGHAM with Court House rock, a landmark on the trail.

OUT ON THE Western plains on her way to Oregon, nineteen-year-old Harriet Talcott Buckingham didn't recognize the flowers she encountered, so she christened one after a novel *The Prairie Flower* by Emerson Bennett. Her "Prairie Flower" may have been a wild morning glory, a hardy little white flower. Today we call them bindweed and have little appreciation for their hardiness, which aggravates both farmer and gardener. But the flowers, which bloom in white or pink, truly thrive in the hot sun and dry winds of the prairie.

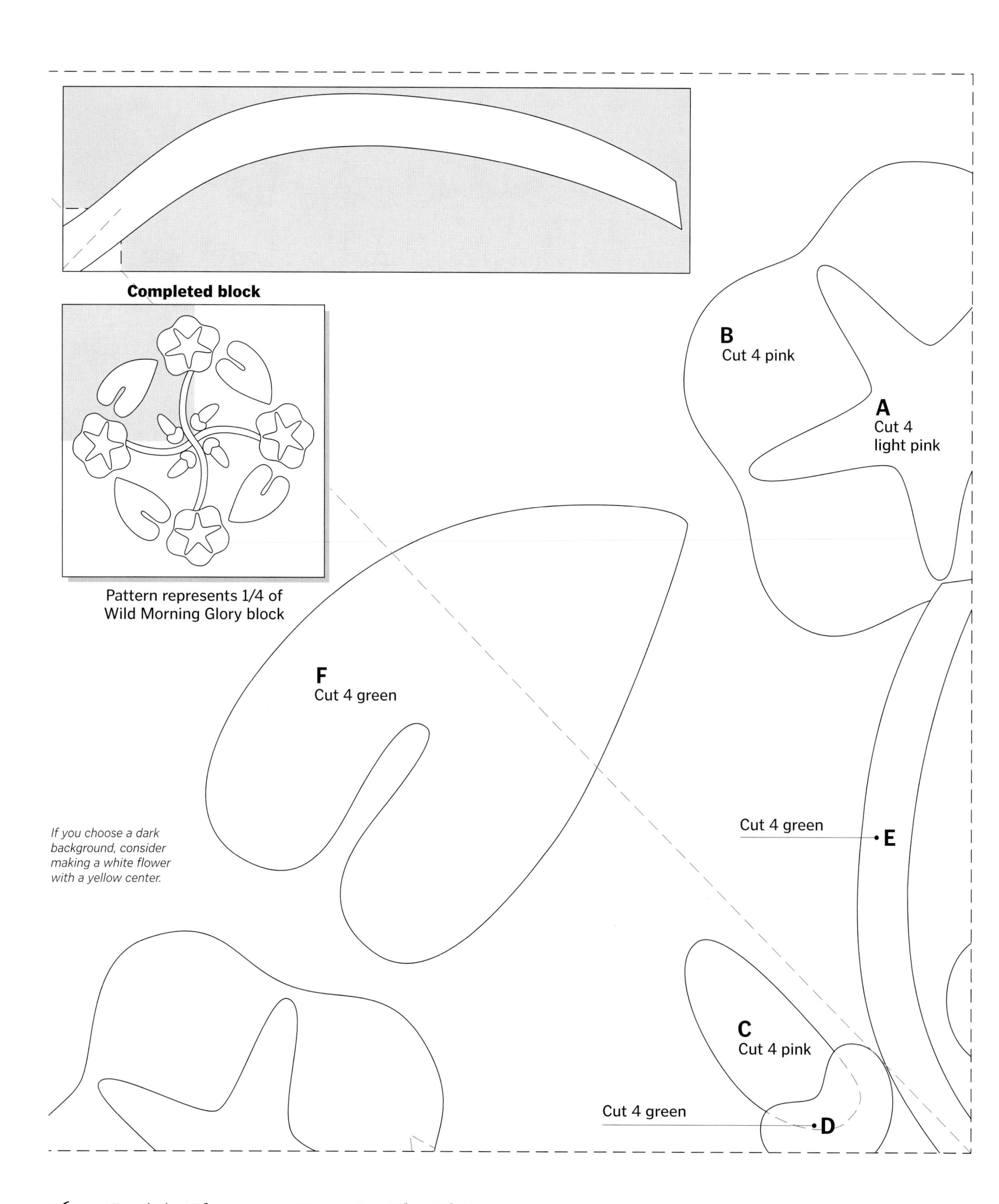

If you choose a dark background, consider making a white flower with a yellow center.

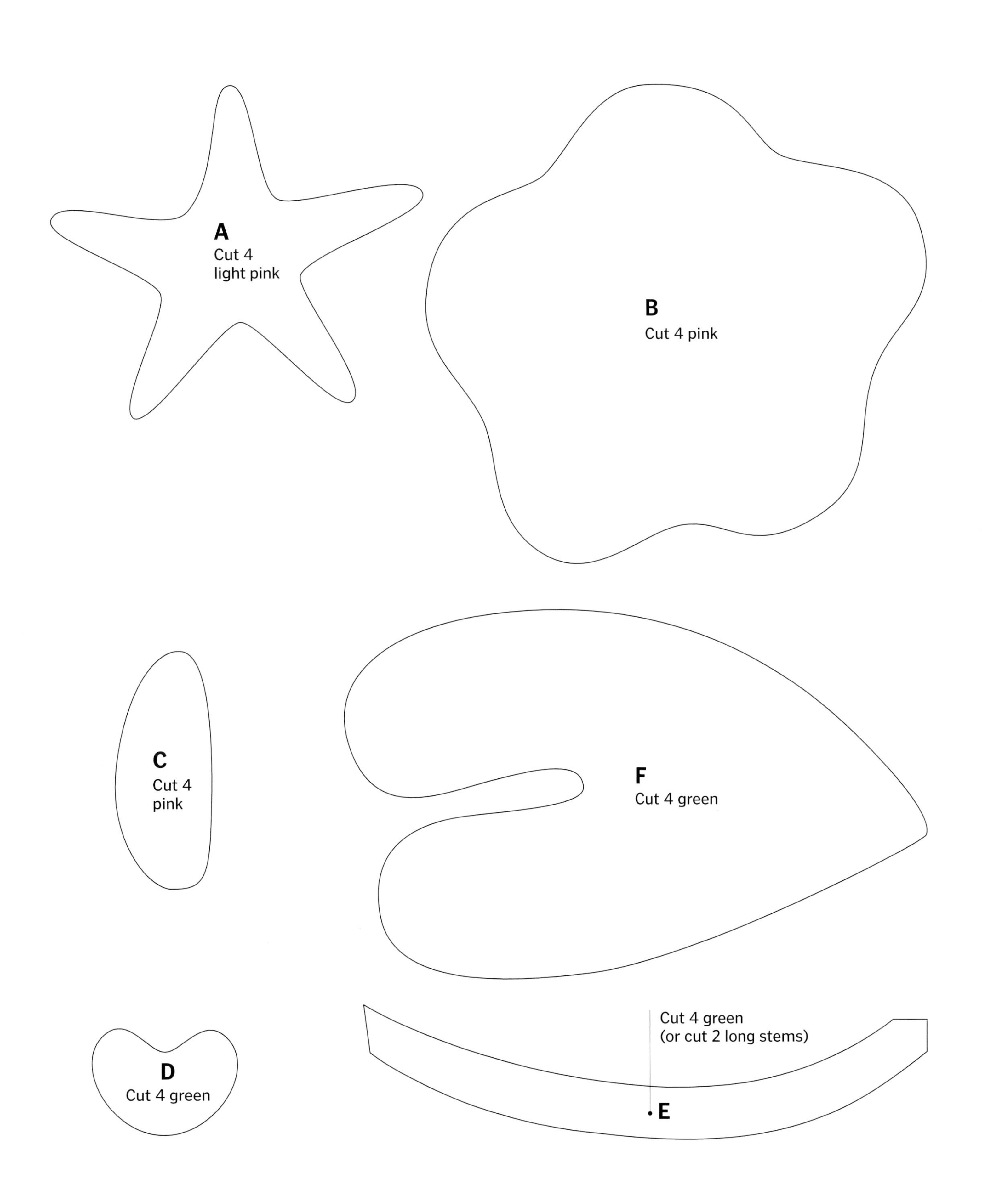
A
Cut 4
light pink
B
Cut 4 pink
C
Cut 4
pink
F
Cut 4 green
D
Cut 4 green
Cut 4 green
(or cut 2 long stems)
E

Sunflower

Common Sunflower, *Helianthus annuus*

SUNFLOWER – block #9

The way she found it...

"July 1st, 1850. The ground is covered with beautifull flowers, it looks like flower gardens. There are immense beds of sun flowers in this reagion, they look like ours at home."

— Lucena Parsons

Hardy women labored willingly to create a home on the harsh prairie, but their journals reveal remembered girlhood. As a child in 1886, Itis Spade shown above came by train from Indiana to Kansas.

The prairie in summer and autumn is abloom in sunflowers. Lucena Parsons, on a journey from Wisconsin to a farm near the Bay in Oakland, Calif., noted one small variety.

The larger plants bloom in the fall and their stalks sometimes last through the winter. Teenager Luna Warner, living on the prairie near Downs, Kan., recorded a day of visiting on an unseasonable December day. "December 2, 1872. Very warm. Vi and I went over to Gena's on horseback. We hitched our horses to sunflowers."

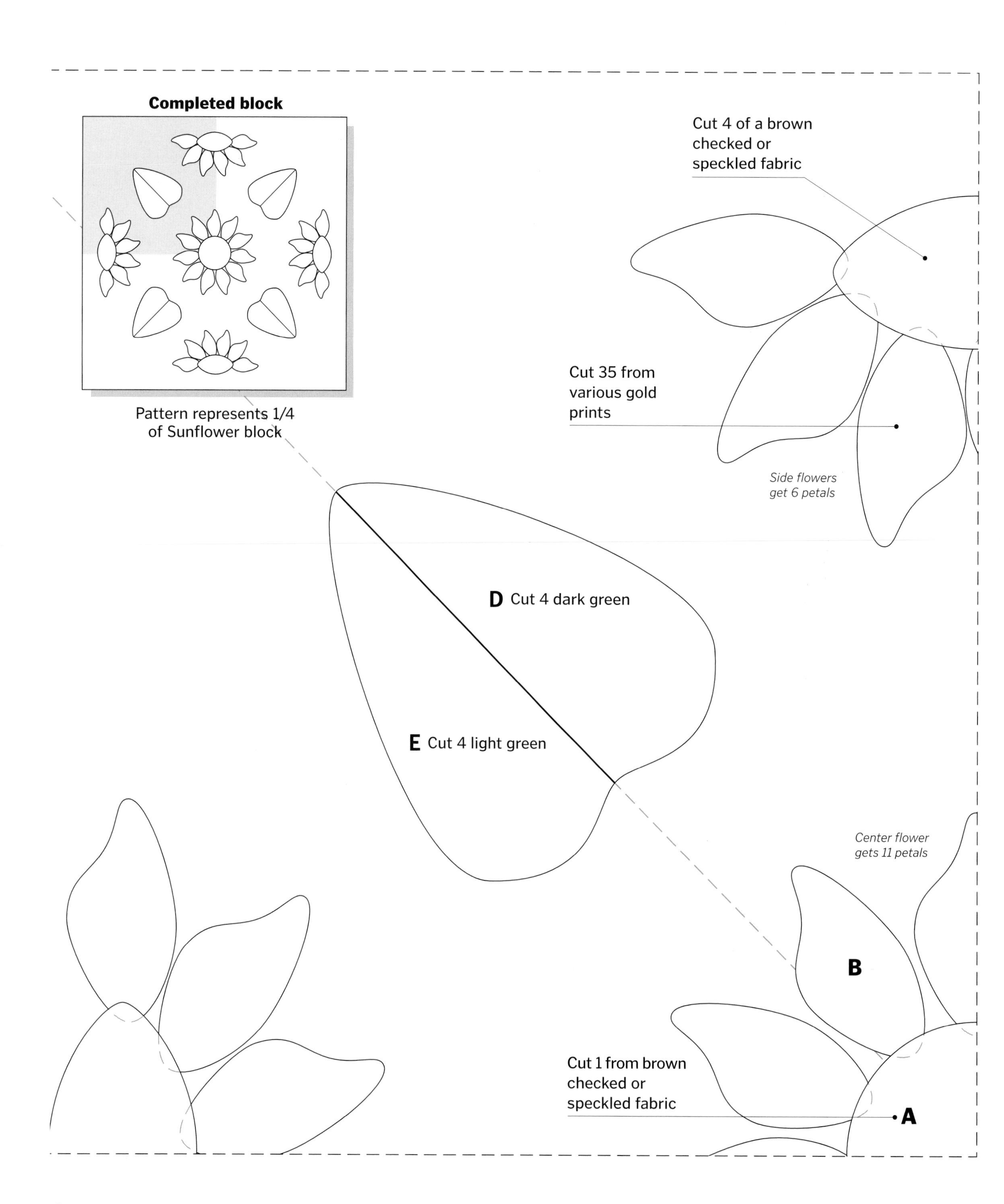
Completed block
Pattern represents 1/4
of Sunflower block
Cut 4 of a brown
checked or
speckled fabric
Cut 35 from
various gold
prints
Side flowers
get 6 petals
D Cut 4 dark green
E Cut 4 light green
Center flower
gets 11 petals
B
Cut 1 from brown
checked or
speckled fabric
A

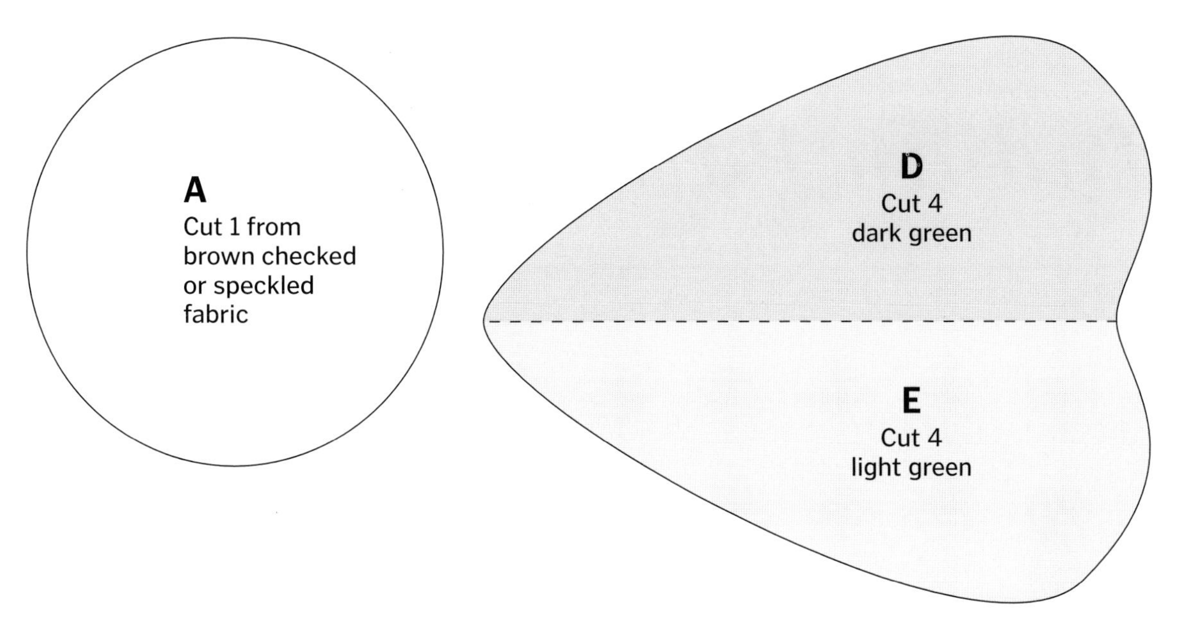

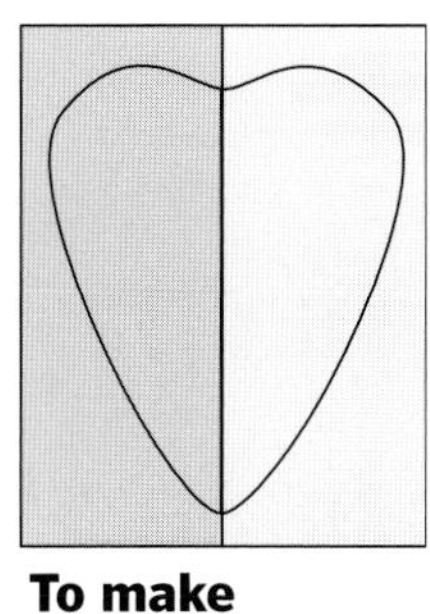

To make leaves:

Cut 2" wide strips (includes seam allowance) of dark and light green, and piece together. Center pattern over seam, trim to size.

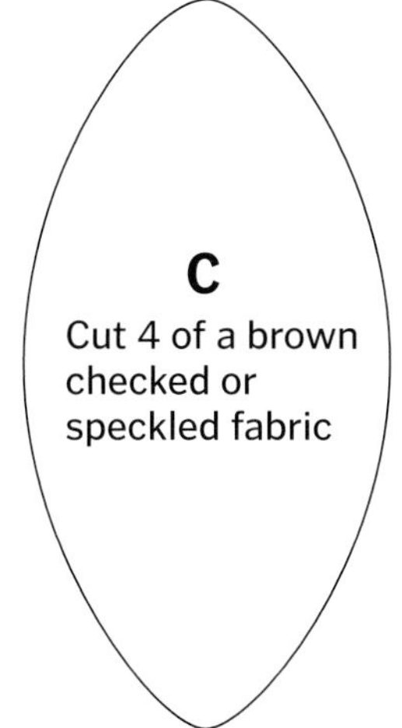

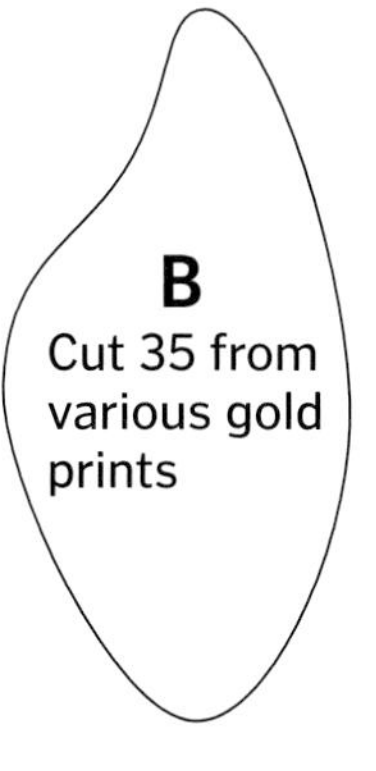

Indian Paintbrush

Castilleja coccinea

Indian Paintbrush– block #10

THE WAY SHE FOUND IT...

"APRIL 28, Let me name some of the flowers I have [seen] within a few days...Indian paint is a name given to a little plant with deep yellow flowers, the juice of the root paints a bright red and is used by the Indians to paint their faces. There is another plant in blossom here which the Indians designate Spring because the juice of its pod furnishes them drink sometimes when traveling where water can not be obtained." —SARAH EVERETT

AFTER YEARS of living in makeshift homes like dugouts and sod-houses, prairie settlers were proud of their new frame houses with all the amenities. Unknown Kansans, about 1910.

SUGARBOWL and creamer, handpainted by Emma Gibbey about 1910.

SARAH EVERETT, who settled near Osawatomie, Kan., in 1856, wrote letters describing the prairies to friends in the East.

Sarah's Indian Paint is not the same plant that we call by that name. When she documented the native tribes' plant lore, she was referring to a functional "paintbrush," whereas our Indian Paintbrush is symbolic, a brushy bright orange plant that reminds us of the days when Kansas was Indian Territory. The red-orange color isn't the flower; it's a leafy bract that encloses a modest little bloom.

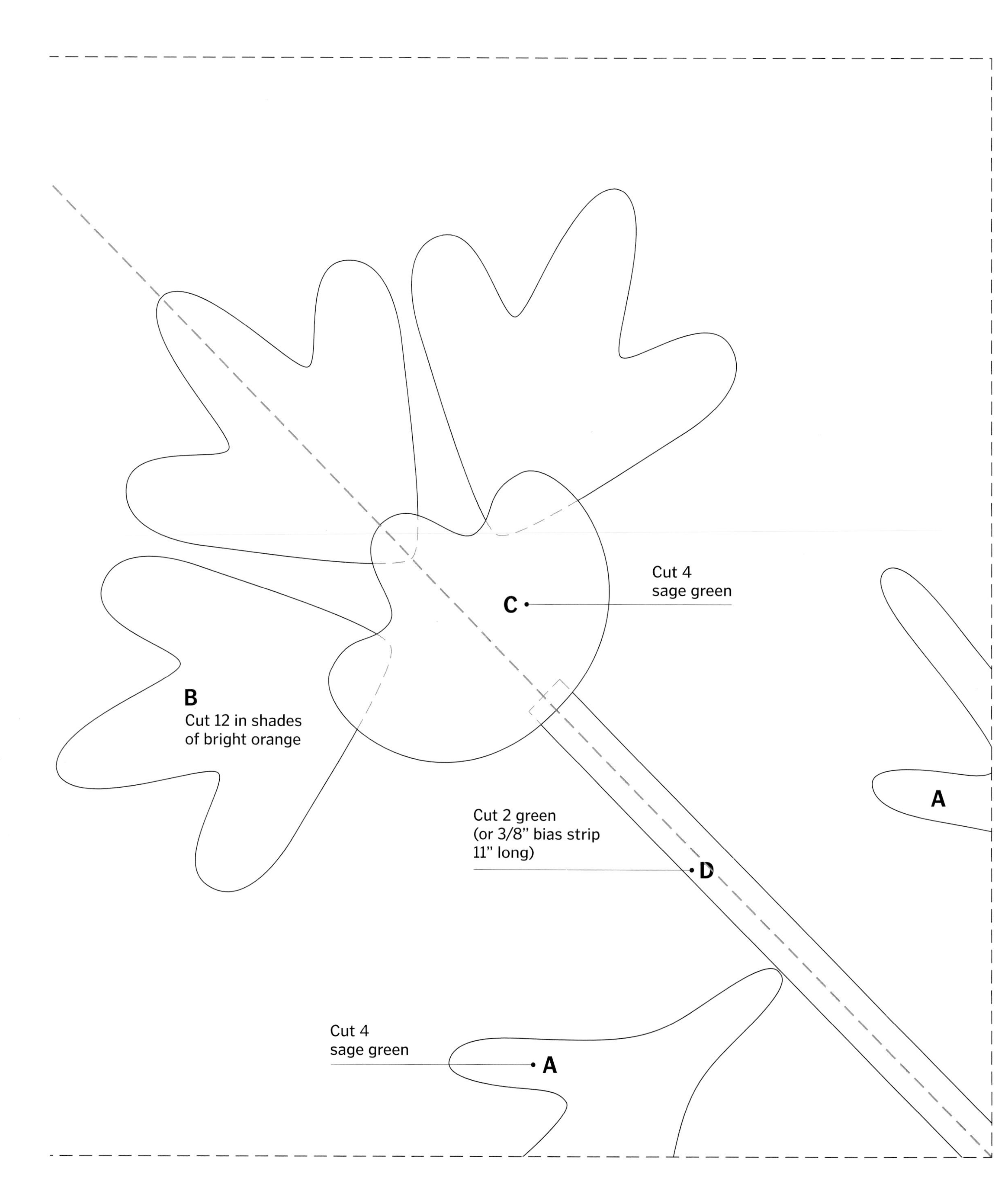
Cut 4
sage green
C
B
Cut 12 in shades
of bright orange
A
Cut 2 green
(or 3/8" bias strip
11" long)
D
Cut 4
sage green
A

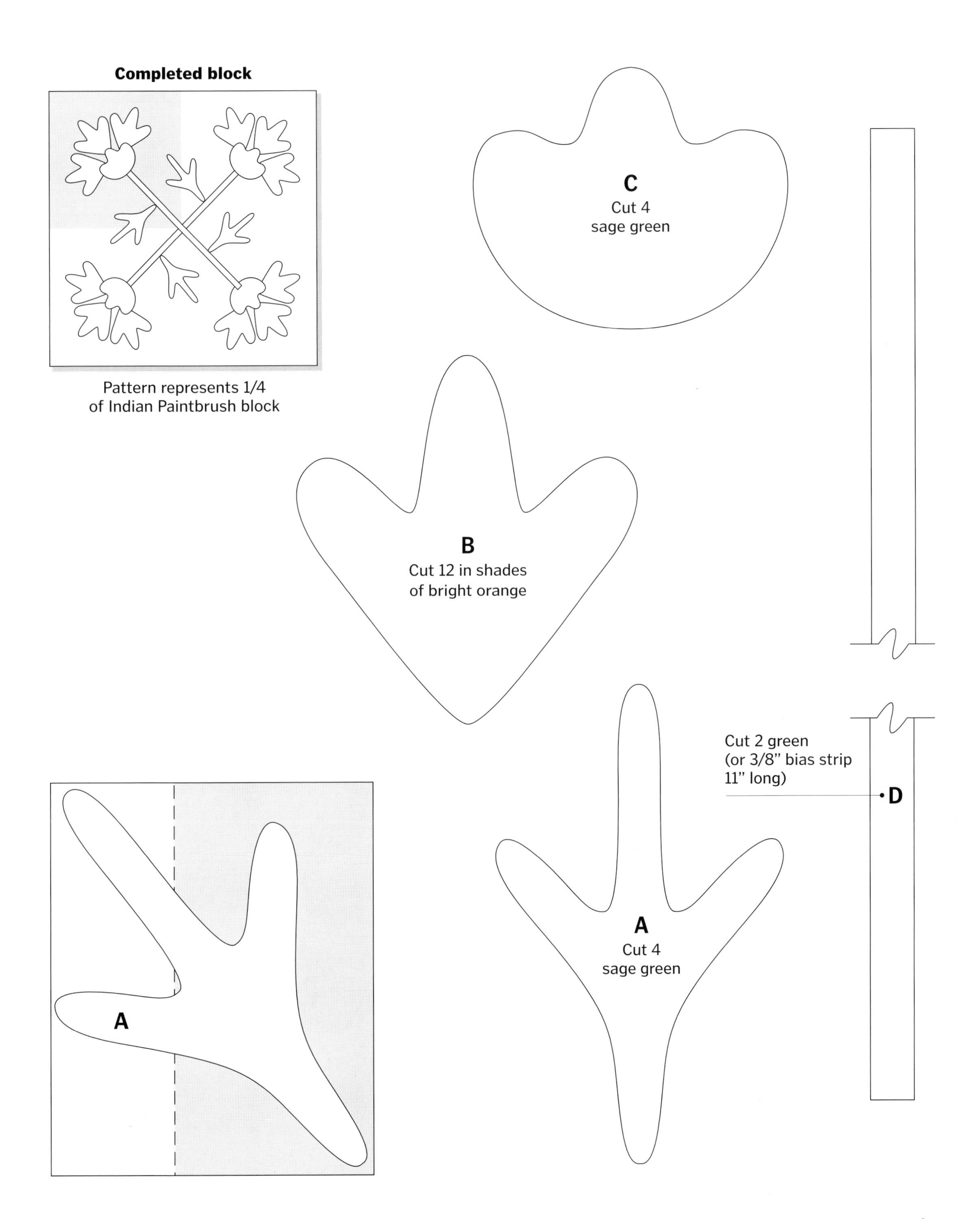
Completed block
Pattern represents 1/4
of Indian Paintbrush block
C
Cut 4
sage green
B
Cut 12 in shades
of bright orange
Cut 2 green
(or 3/8" bias strip
11" long)
D
A
Cut 4
sage green
A

Aster

Willow Aster, *Aster praealtus*

ASTER– block #11

The Way She Found It...

"June 23, 1852. This section of country is all sandy soil and where the bluffs run near the river we find deep sand. We find numerous kinds of flowers. A great many of them resemble our tame flowers such as fox glove, lark spur, rose moss, china oyster....We have not much to attract our attention but flowers and the bluffs in some places are quite a curiosity."

—Martha S. Thompson Read

Housework, cooking, laundry, gardens and the chicken coop were the domestic sphere of the farm wife. Unknown woman about 1920.

Asters were cultivated in the Eastern United States from Colonial days. Gardeners sent species around the world, with American asters delighting the English and China Asters growing in American gardens decades before our Revolution. Women crossing the prairies recognized the wild Prairie Asters, Willow Asters and Blue Asters as relatives of the cultivated species. Martha S. Thompson Read wrote about familiar flowers in her diary. On the way from Massachusetts to Oregon she recorded the sights on the trail one day west of Chimney Rock in what is now Nebraska. Martha, who had just turned forty-one, seemed to know a bit about horticulture, if less about spelling "oyster" vs. "aster."

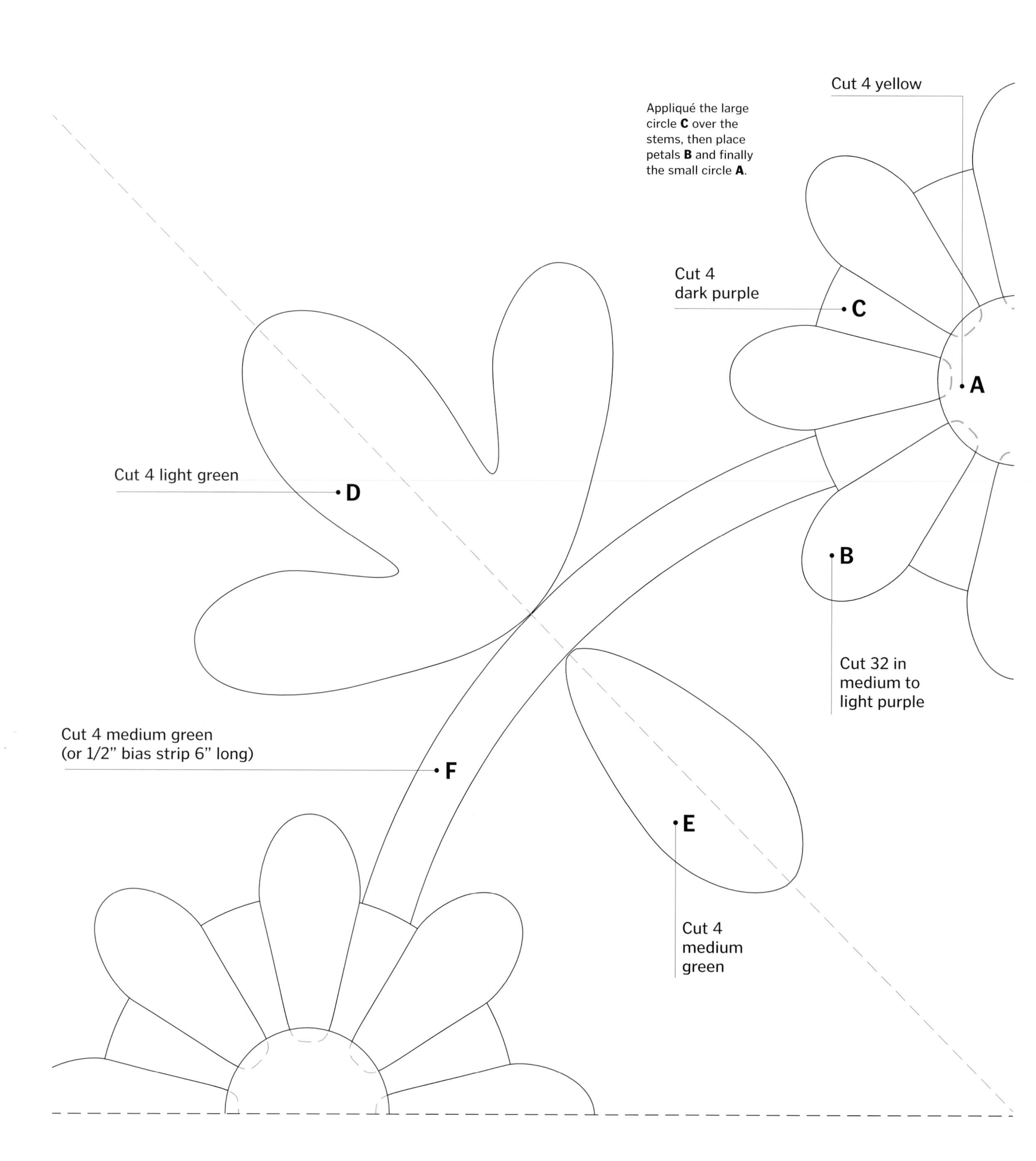
Cut 4 yellow
Appliqué the large circle **C** over the stems, then place petals **B** and finally the small circle **A**.
Cut 4 dark purple
C
A
Cut 4 light green
D
B
Cut 32 in medium to light purple
Cut 4 medium green (or 1/2" bias strip 6" long)
F
E
Cut 4 medium green

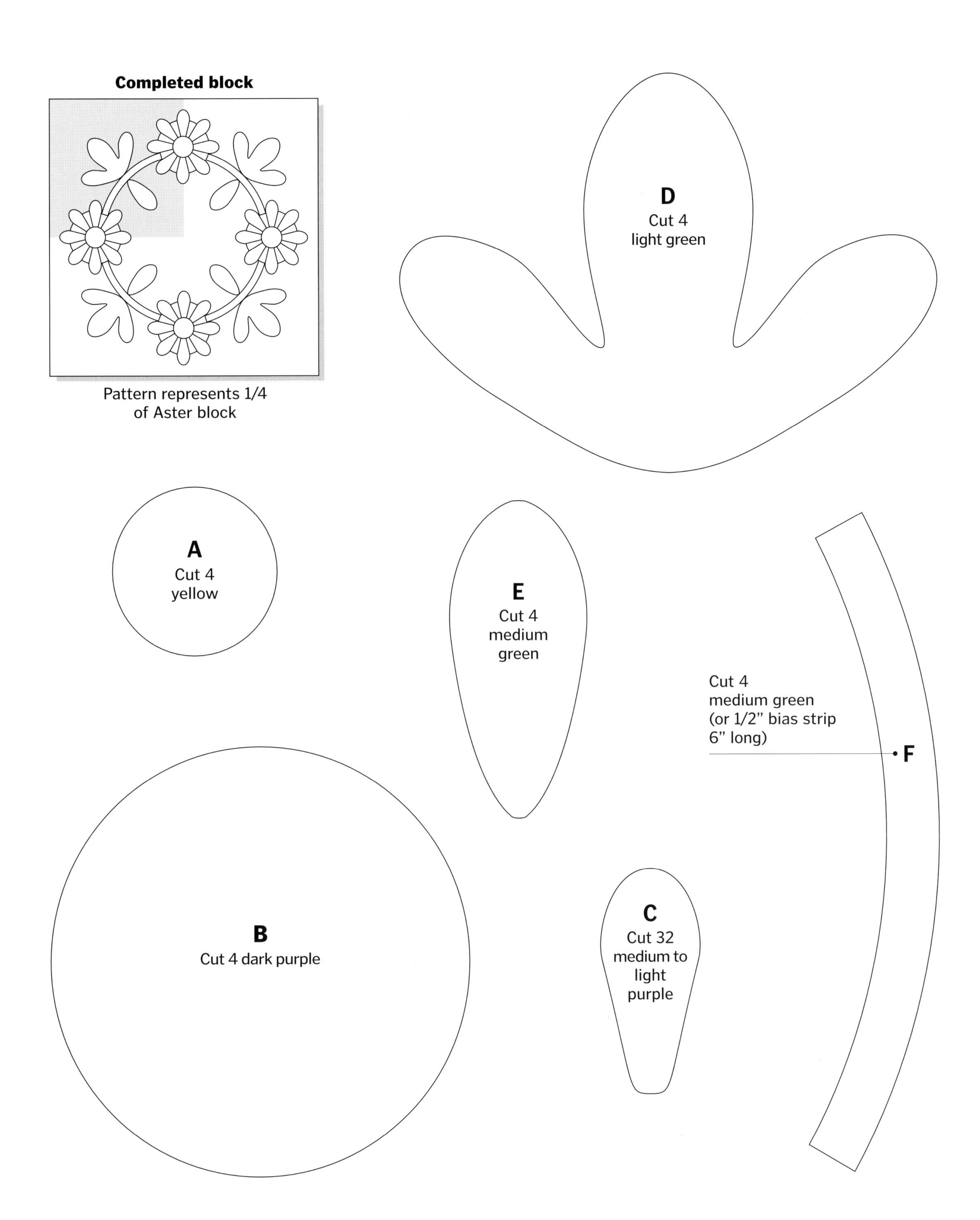
Completed block
Pattern represents 1/4
of Aster block
D
Cut 4
light green
A
Cut 4
yellow
E
Cut 4
medium
green
Cut 4
medium green
(or 1/2" bias strip
6" long)
F
B
Cut 4 dark purple
C
Cut 32
medium to
light
purple

Johnny-Jump-Up

Viola rafinesquii

Johnny-Jump-Up– block #12

THE WAY SHE FOUND IT...

"How we did laugh, but we laughed more yet, when some time later he said, 'I remember now, it is the Johny jump up." —Abbie Bright

Abbie Bright shared laughter with Cousin Jim about "Johnny-Jump-Ups."

Abbie Bright came west to homestead in 1870. On the trip from Pennsylvania to join her brother near Clearwater, Kan., she stopped to visit her cousins. On April 7, a "fine day" in Illinois, she noticed some wild rose canes and asked cousin Jim, who lived there, what color the blooms would be. Jim said "he had never noticed, and when I asked the name of a shrub with a yellow fringe of bloom, he said. 'I can't tell you, really I only know the name of one flower.' 'What is that,' I asked. Then he could not remember it. How we did laugh, but we laughed more yet, when some time later he said, 'I remember now, it is the Johny jump up.'"

"Johnny-jump-up" is a name still given to a wide variety of violas or little violets that pop up so quickly in the spring. Abbie probably came across them on her Kansas claim. Clara Conron, who lived near Topeka, noted them in her 1884 diary. "April 26, This p.m. Nellie took a walk to look for Johnny Jump-Ups ... found quite a good many."

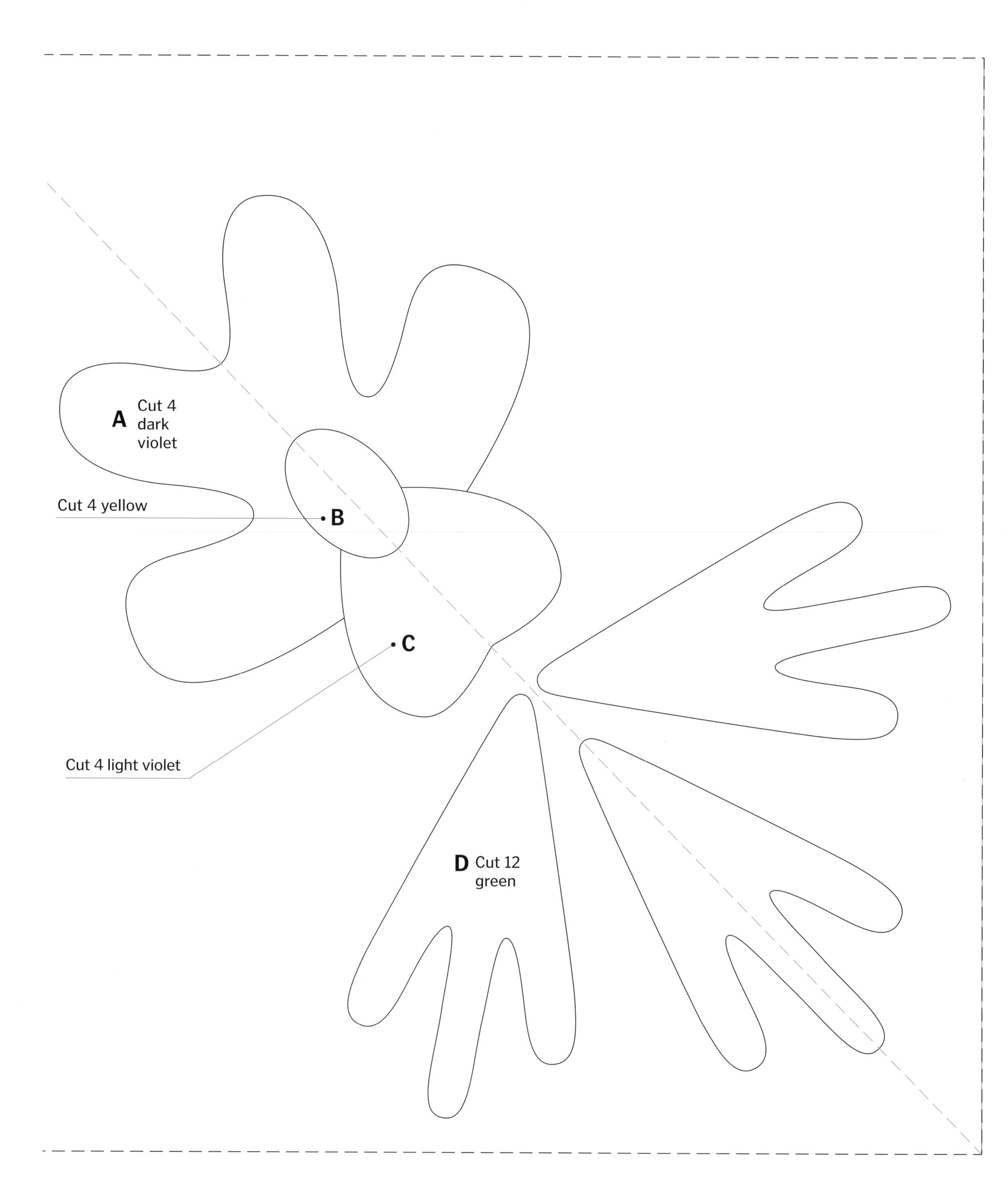
A Cut 4 dark violet
Cut 4 yellow
B
C
Cut 4 light violet
D Cut 12 green

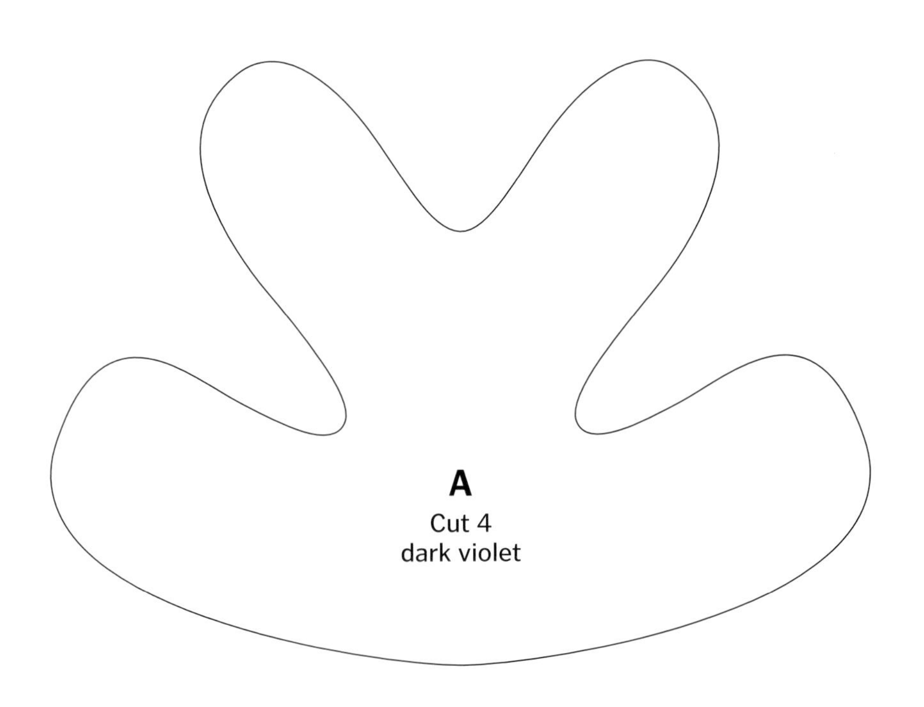

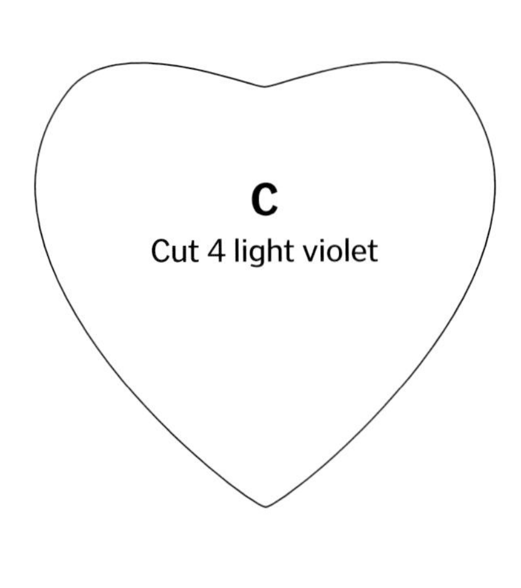

B
Cut 4 yellow

Completed block

Pattern represents 1/4
of Johnny-Jump-Up block

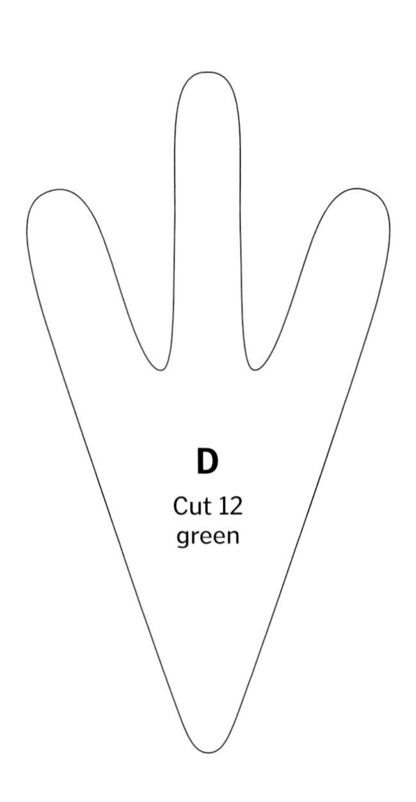

The Heart of the Matter

SETTING, BORDERS, QUILTING & BINDING

SETTING THE BLOCKS

We are giving you two settings, but as you can see from the photographs, you have many options and can invent your own. The appliqué blocks are of two main design types, X's and O's. The X blocks (Bittersweet, Dandelion, Sweet William, Wild Cucumber, Missouri Primrose, Indian Paintbrush) extend into the corners of the blocks. The O blocks (Sorrel, Wild Rose, Morning Glory, Sunflower, Aster, Johnny Jump Up) have rather empty corners. Alternate X's and O's to get a balanced look.

As you lay out, focus on balanced color. Scatter the yellow blocks throughout since yellow tends to jump out. Avoid clumping the purple flowers in one area and the pinks in another. Don't worry about identical background fabrics touching. You are bound to have identical fabrics side by side. Backgrounds are not as important as balancing the color and the X's and O's.

Rectangular Quilt (A)

Our first setting option is a rectangle of the 12 wildflowers, set in four rows of three. Trim your blocks to 18 1/2" so your finished blocks are 18" square. The top with no borders will measure 54 1/2" x 72 1/2" with the seam allowances. You may then choose from our three border options: plain (Border #1), Sawtooth (Border #2) and Appliquéd Vine (Border #3).

Square Quilt (B)

Some people prefer a square quilt, so we have included an extra basket block, which is to be repeated four times for the corners. (See page 76.) Set the blocks in four rows of four, as shown. The pieced basket fits into the top of the corner blocks so that the appliquéd border grows out of the basket. Trim your blocks to 18 1/2" so your finished blocks are 18" square. The square top with no borders will measure 72 1/2" x 72 1/2" with seam allowances. See the Appliquéd Vine Border (Border #3) on page 81.

Prairie Flower, machine appliquéd by Jean Stanclift, Lawrence, Kan.; machine quilted by Rosie Mayhew, Topeka, Kan. I picked the fabrics for Jean to appliqué in this quilt, which uses the four extra basket blocks and the Appliquéd Vine Border. Rosie machine quilted her own choice of feathers in the corners and border.

(A) Rectangular block setting

(B) Square block setting

The Basket Blocks

18” finished

Fabric Requirements

For the large triangles and the baskets: 1 1/4 yards of background fabric

For the dark basket pieces: 1 fat quarter. Because there is so much going on in this quilt I thought the baskets should be subtle, so we chose a print just a little bit darker than the background.

Scraps for the Bittersweet appliqué.

Cutting:

Cut and prepare for appliqué 24 Bittersweet berries (see page 26).

For the large triangles (E) under the baskets, cut two squares 19”. Cut each on the diagonal into two triangles. You'll have four triangles, one for each of the baskets.

For the smaller triangles (A), cut two squares 9 7/8”. Again cut each on the diagonal into two triangles. You'll have the triangles for the top of the baskets.

For the triangles (D), cut four squares 9 7/8”. Cut each square diagonally into two triangles. You will cover the corners of these triangles with the small triangle B as shown to make the base of each basket.

For the checks in the basket you can use the templates or these rotary cutting instructions.

Cut 2” squares. You'll need 9 light and 6 dark for each basket, or 36 light and 24 dark in all.

Cut 2 3/8” squares out of the darker fabric for the triangles. Cut these in half diagonally, making two triangles from each square. You'll need three squares (8 triangles) for each basket, making 16 squares or 32 dark triangles in all.

Sewing

Piece a triangle B over the edge of the larger triangle D. Piece strips of squares and triangles as shown into the basket. Add triangle A to the basket. You may want to leave gaps in this seam for now, so you can tuck the stems in later.

Then add triangles D.

Finally add the largest triangle E.

Appliqué three Bittersweet berries on the sides of each basket as shown.

Leave the top of one berry open so you can add the stems after

Corner basket squares

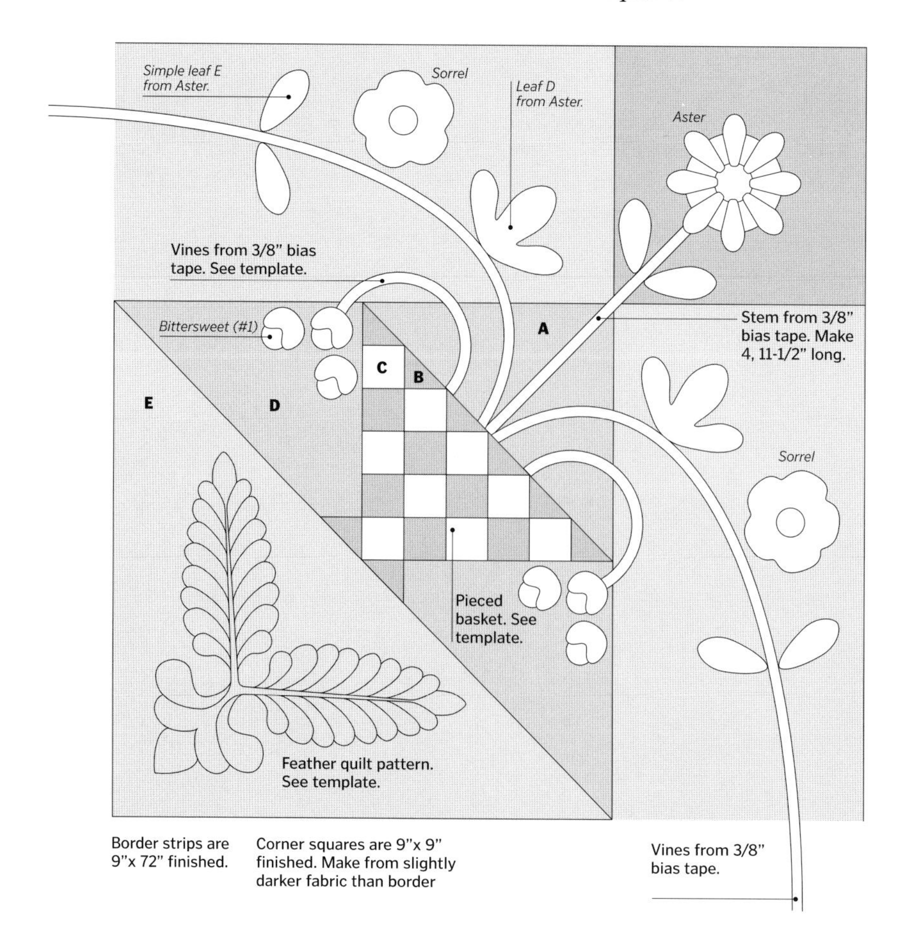

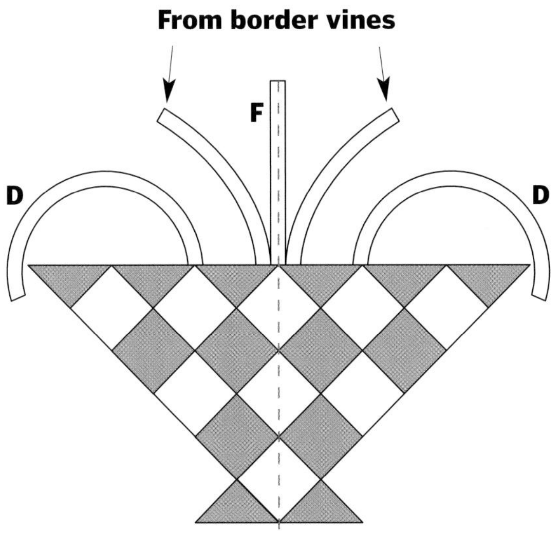

From border vines

F

D

D

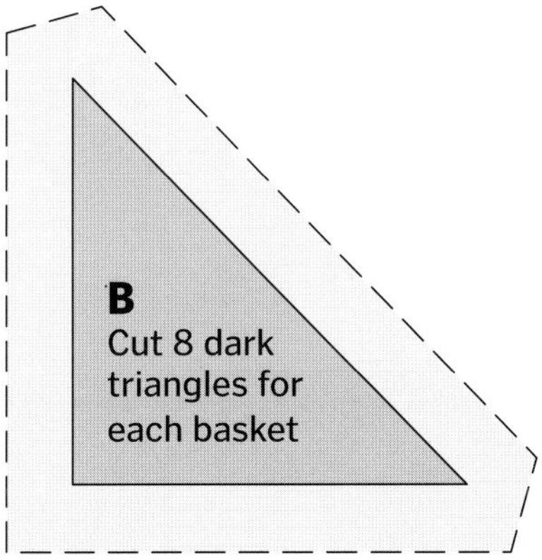

B
Cut 8 dark triangles for each basket

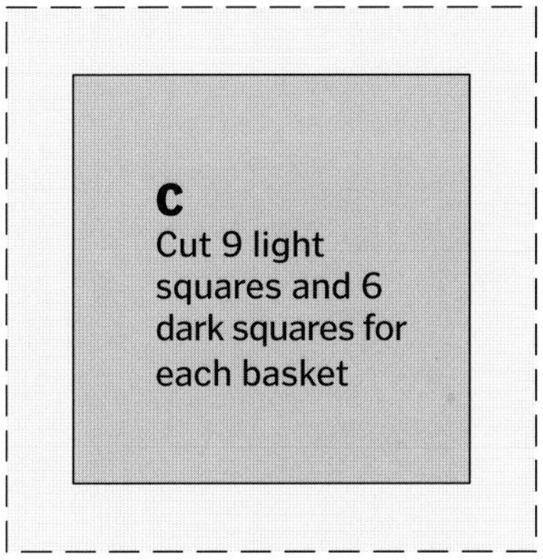

C
Cut 9 light squares and 6 dark squares for each basket

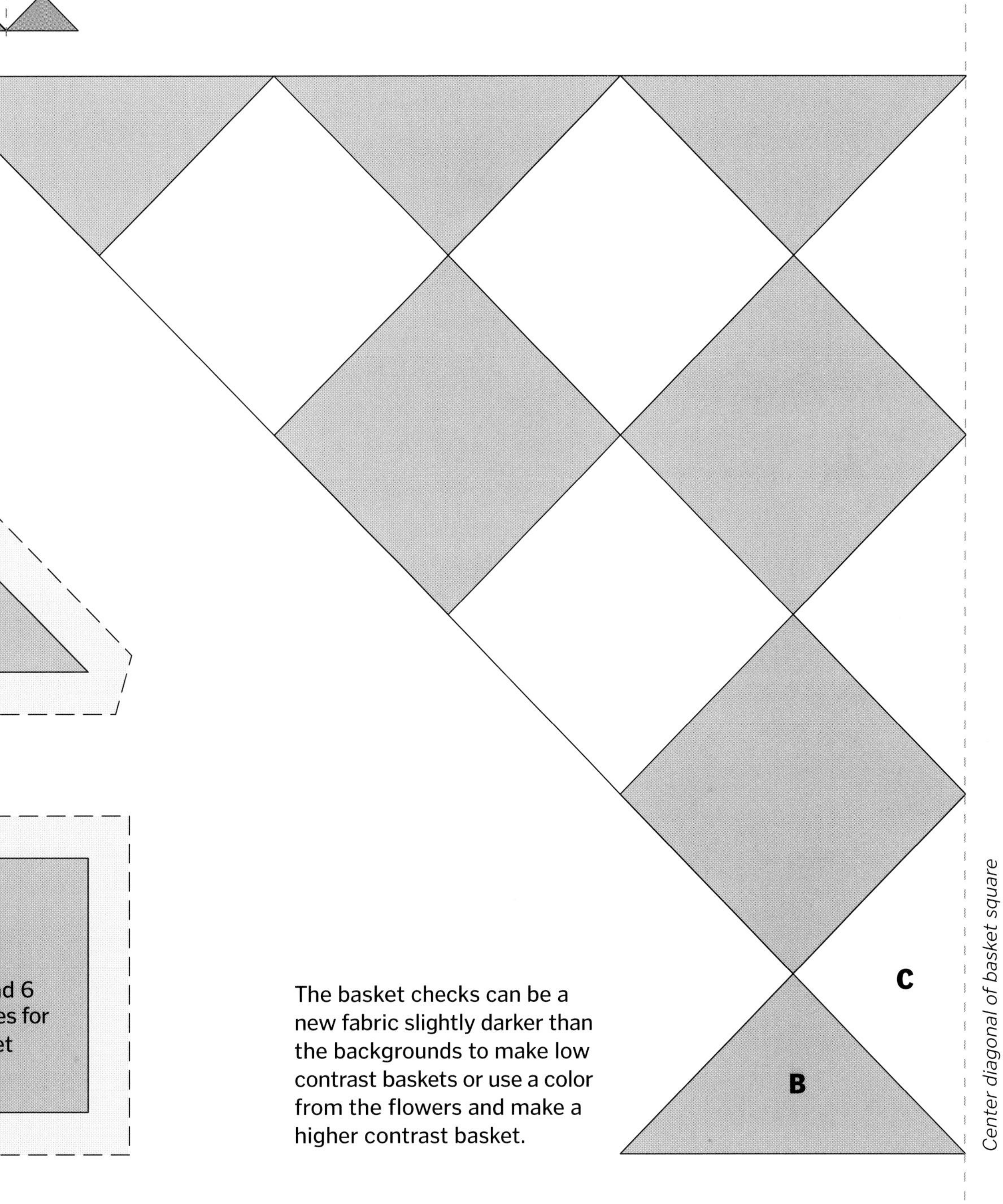

The basket checks can be a new fabric slightly darker than the backgrounds to make low contrast baskets or use a color from the flowers and make a higher contrast basket.

C

B

Center diagonal of basket square

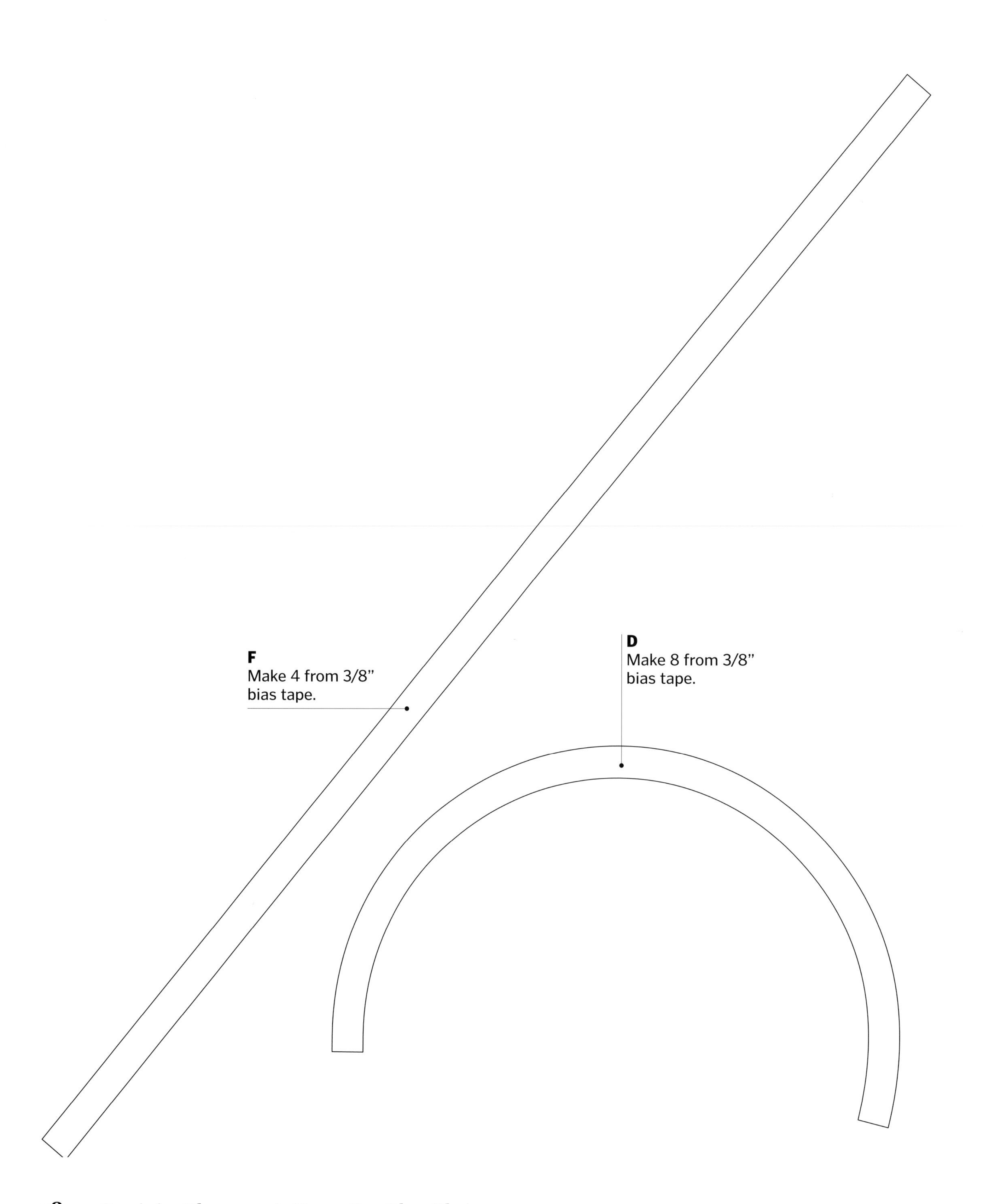
F
Make 4 from 3/8"
bias tape.
D
Make 8 from 3/8"
bias tape.

SPRING PRAIRIE FLOWERS, hand appliquéd by Rosalyn Douglass, Overland Park, Kan., unquilted top. Rosalyn used the simple border #1 for her study in soft colors.

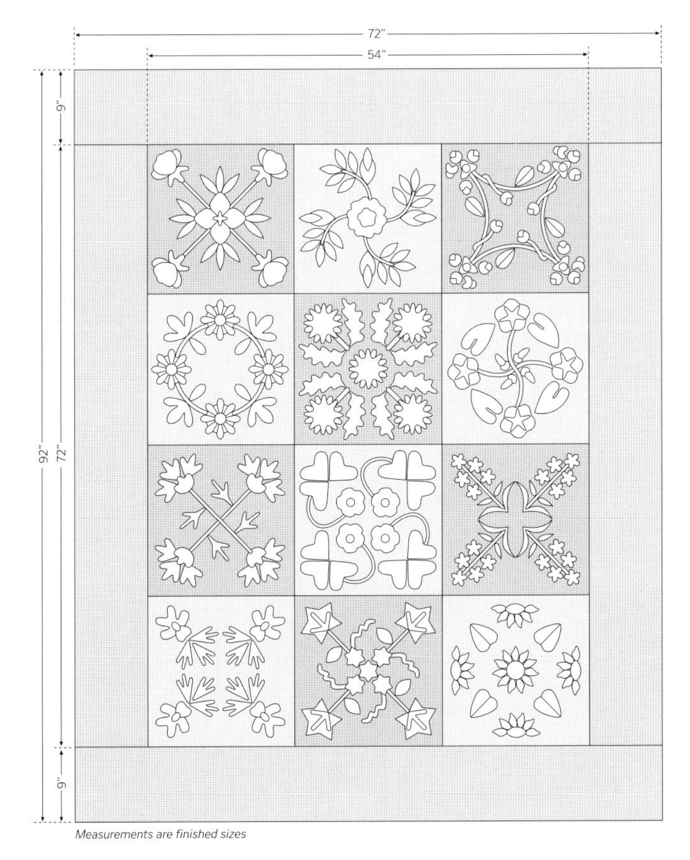

PLAIN (Border #1)

you've added the border.

This might be a good time to trace the Feather and Fleur-de-lis quilting design (see page 86) onto the large triangle E while the blocks are easy to handle.

BORDERS

For the rectangular set, you have three border options: Plain (Border #1), Sawtooth (Border #2) and Appliquéd Vine (Border #3).

PLAIN BORDER #1

72" x 90" quilt

Fabric Requirements:

You'll need 2 1/4 yards for this border. You may want to use one of the background fabrics for this border, as Rosalyn Douglass has. You can also use something a little darker, so the border frames the blocks.

Cutting & Sewing

Cut 4 strips 9 1/2" x 72 1/2" (includes seam allowance).

Seam one strip to each side; then add the top and bottom strips as shown.

SAWTOOTH BORDER #2

74" x 92" Quilt

You'll be adding three borders, one at a time.

Fabric Requirements:

For the two plain borders you'll need 2 3/4 yards of background fabric to cut into strips.

PRAIRIE FLOWER, hand appliqued by Barbara Brackman, Lawrence, Kan., unquilted top. Jean Stanclift pieced the sawtooth border (#2), using scraps from the backgrounds and appliqué. These are the blocks I used to design the quilt for the newspaper - my first draft, so to speak.

For the sawtooth border, you'll need background fabric equivalent to a rectangle about 40" x 20" (3/4 yard of fabric). For a scrappy look, though, you may want to cut these triangles from the leftovers of your background fabrics.

You'll need a contrasting color of the same size (3/4 yard). Again, you will probably want to cut these triangles from the appliqué leftovers, as I did in the sample.

Cutting, Sewing Plain Strips

The inner border is a plain 3" border. Cut 2 strips 3 1/2" x 72 1/2" for the sides. Seam one to each side first.

Cut 2 strips 3 1/2" x 60 1/2" for the top and bottom borders. Add these.

Cutting, Sewing Sawtooth Strips

For the corners of this border, you'll need four squares finishing to 3". So cut 3 1/2" squares with the seam allowance included.

For the triangles, the sawteeth, cut 3" finished triangles, using either the template (page 81) or rotary cutting instructions. You will need 90 light triangles and 90 dark triangles to piece into the sawtooth squares.

Piece the sawtooth squares into strips. You'll need: 2 strips of 20 sawtooth squares for the top and bottom borders (with seams these strips will be 3 1/2" x 60 1/2"). Seam these to the top and bottom of the quilt first. Two strips of 25

SAWTOOTH (Border #2)

Rotary cutting triangles:
Cut strips 3-7/8" wide
Cut squares 3-7/8"
Cut into 2 diagonally

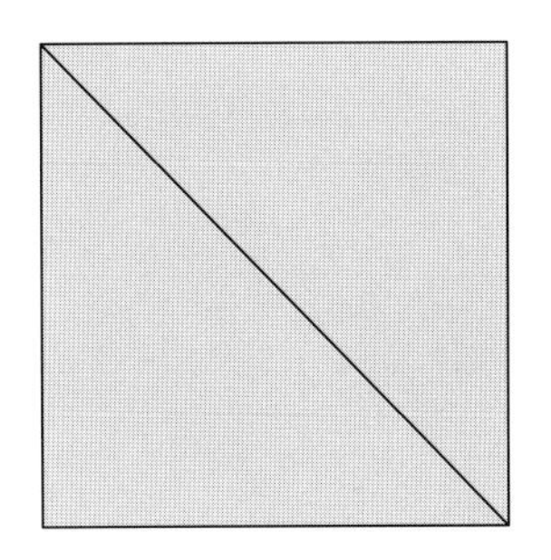

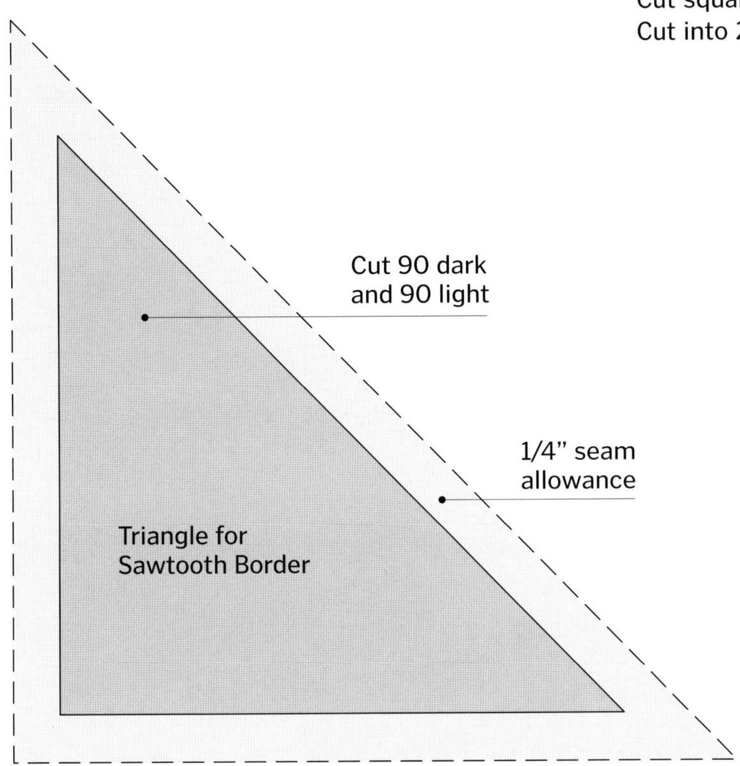

sawtooth squares for the side borders (with seams these strips will be 3 1/2" x 78 1/2"). Add the corner squares to the ends, making strips 84 1/2" long. Add them to the quilt as shown.

Cutting, Sewing Outer Strips

The outer border is a plain 4" border.

Cut two strips 4 1/2" x 84 1/2" for the sides. Seam these to the sides first.

Cut two strips 4 1/2" x 72 1/2" for the top and bottom borders. Add these last

Your quilt is now 72" x 92". You might want to add another 6" border to the sides to make it squarer - 84" x 92".

Appliqué Vine Border (#3)

You can add the Appliquéd Vine border to the rectangular or the square set.

Fabric Requirements

When Jean Stanclift and I were working on this quilt, we had no idea where we were going. As with many block-of-the-month projects, the designers are as surprised as the readers, because we worked just a few weeks ahead of the deadline. Of course, I hadn't bought enough background fabric and when we went shopping for more – well, you know the story.

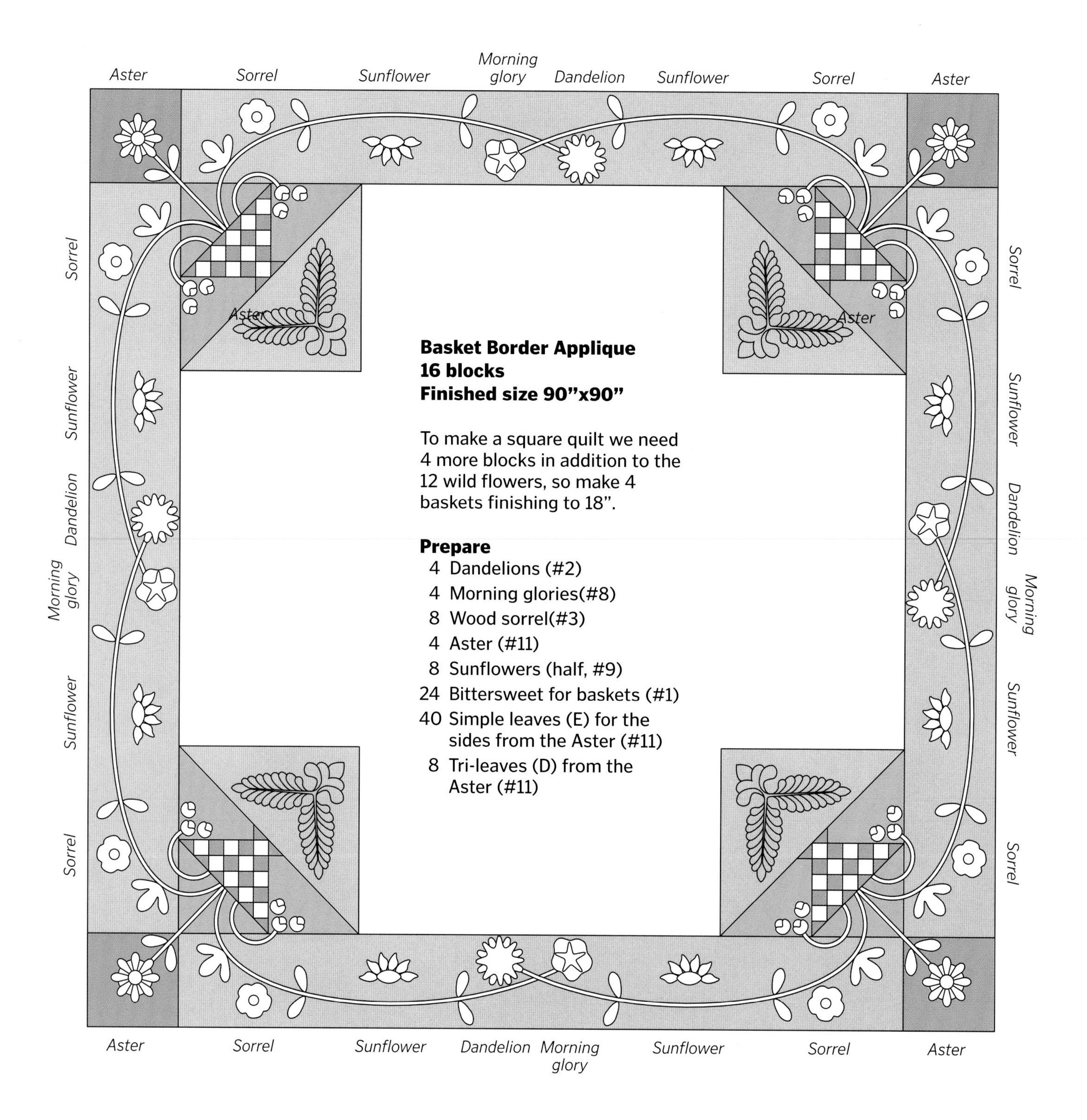

Basket Border Applique
16 blocks
Finished size 90"x90"

To make a square quilt we need 4 more blocks in addition to the 12 wild flowers, so make 4 baskets finishing to 18".

Prepare

- 4 Dandelions (#2)
- 4 Morning glories(#8)
- 8 Wood sorrel(#3)
- 4 Aster (#11)
- 8 Sunflowers (half, #9)
- 24 Bittersweet for baskets (#1)
- 40 Simple leaves (E) for the sides from the Aster (#11)
- 8 Tri-leaves (D) from the Aster (#11)

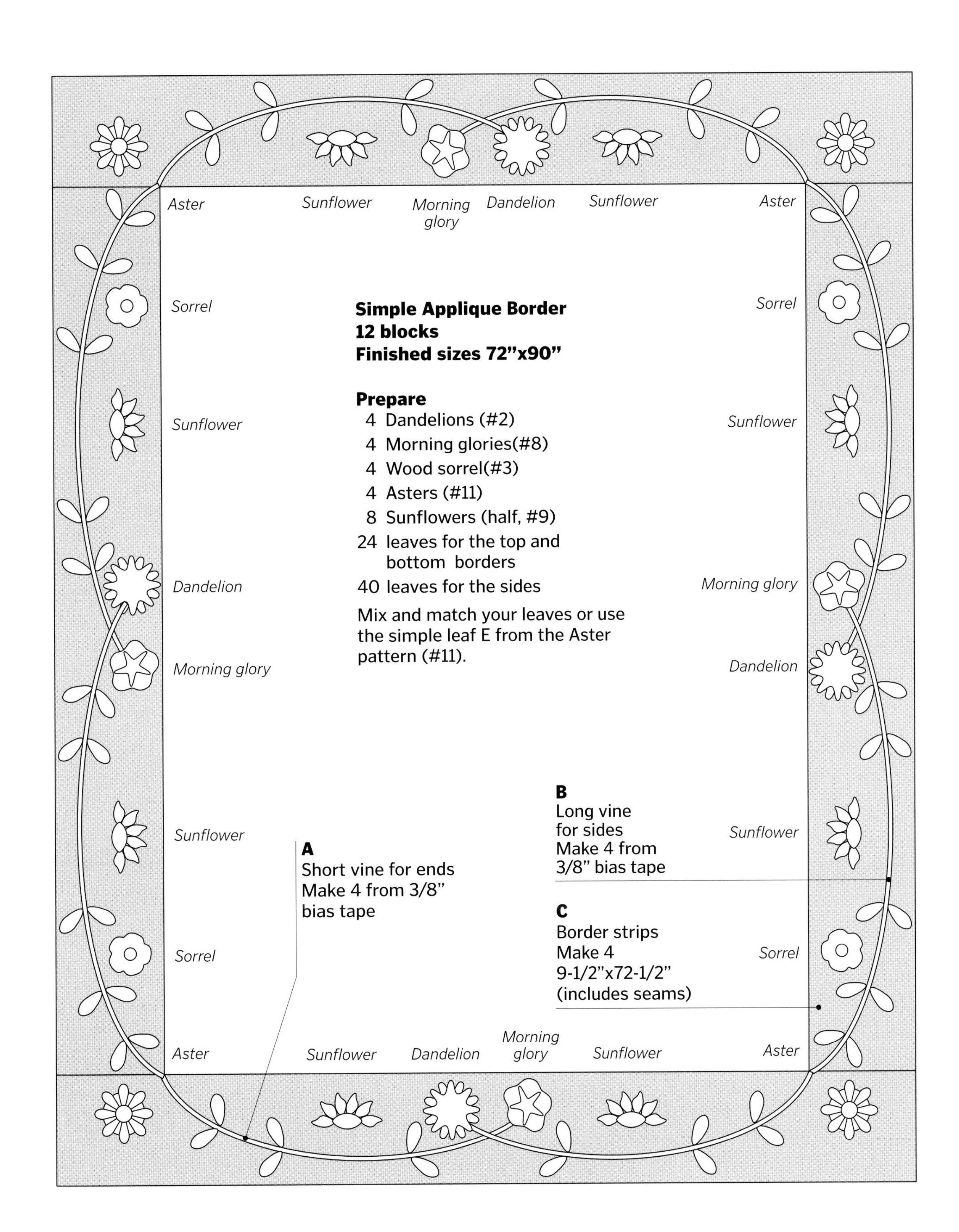
Aster
Sunflower
Morning glory
Dandelion
Sunflower
Aster
Sorrel
Sorrel
Simple Applique Border
12 blocks
Finished sizes 72"x90"
Prepare
4 Dandelions (#2)
4 Morning glories(#8)
4 Wood sorrel(#3)
4 Asters (#11)
8 Sunflowers (half, #9)
24 leaves for the top and bottom borders
40 leaves for the sides
Mix and match your leaves or use the simple leaf E from the Aster pattern (#11).
Sunflower
Sunflower
Dandelion
Morning glory
Morning glory
Dandelion
B
Long vine for sides
Make 4 from 3/8" bias tape
Sunflower
A
Short vine for ends
Make 4 from 3/8" bias tape
Sunflower
C
Border strips
Make 4
9-1/2"x72-1/2"
(includes seams)
Sorrel
Sorrel
Aster
Sunflower
Dandelion
Morning glory
Sunflower
Aster

So we had to be flexible and use contrasting shades of new prints that we hadn't used in the wildflower blocks.

Running out of fabric often makes a quilt more interesting than one where the colors are quite controlled. You can copy our mix-and-match color scheme, or plan ahead by buying extra yardage of the background fabrics for the basket blocks and the borders.

2 3/4 yards of background fabric for strips

2/3 of a yard for the corner squares (we used a darker fabric, which we also used in the baskets).

1/2 yard of green cut into 3/8" bias strips for the vine for the rectangular border (8 yards of bias) OR 3/4 yards of green cut into 3/8" bias strips for the vine for the square border (14 yards of bias)

Scraps of the fabric used in the appliqué blocks for the flowers and leaves

Cutting the Strips

Cut four 9 1/2" squares for the border corners, which will finish to 9"

Cut four strips 9 1/2" by 72 1/2"

Appliquéing the Border

The border features several of my favorite wild flowers from the blocks. You'll need to cut pieces for the following flowers and leaves:

4 Dandelions (see page 30)

4 Morning Glories (see page 54)

8 Wood Sorrel (see page 34)

4 Asters (see page 66)

8 Sunflowers-the half Sunflowers (see page 58)

32 Simple Leaves (see leaf E from the Aster, page 66)

8 Triple Leaves (see leaf D from the Aster page 66)

VINE Border (#3), Square setting

VINE Border (#3), Rectangular setting

Finish sewing the appliqué in the borders before you attach the borders. Prepare each flower for appliqué. Reserve the four Asters and position the other flowers to the background strips with pins or water soluble glue as shown. Then connect the flowers with the bias vine, making gentle curves as shown. For the square quilt, leave extra vine in the corners to curve into the basket blocks. Then add the leaves in appropriate places, reserving the eight leaves for the corner blocks until later.

Stitch down everything. For the square quilt, leave the vines that curve into the corners to appliqué later.

Seam the two side strips to the quilt top.

The corner blocks

Place the asters as shown. If you are doing the rectangular quilt, you can omit the stem. Otherwise, appliqué the stem for the square quilt, and leave a good deal of stem hanging off the corner. Add the leaves. Then add the corner blocks to the top and bottom strips. Add those top and bottom borders to your quilt top.

For the square quilt, finish positioning the vines in the corners now. Curve the vines toward the baskets and tuck them into or over the seam. Make stems for the Bittersweet and curve them into or over the seam as shown. Tuck the other edge of that stem in the spot you left open on the Bittersweet berry. Stitch down.

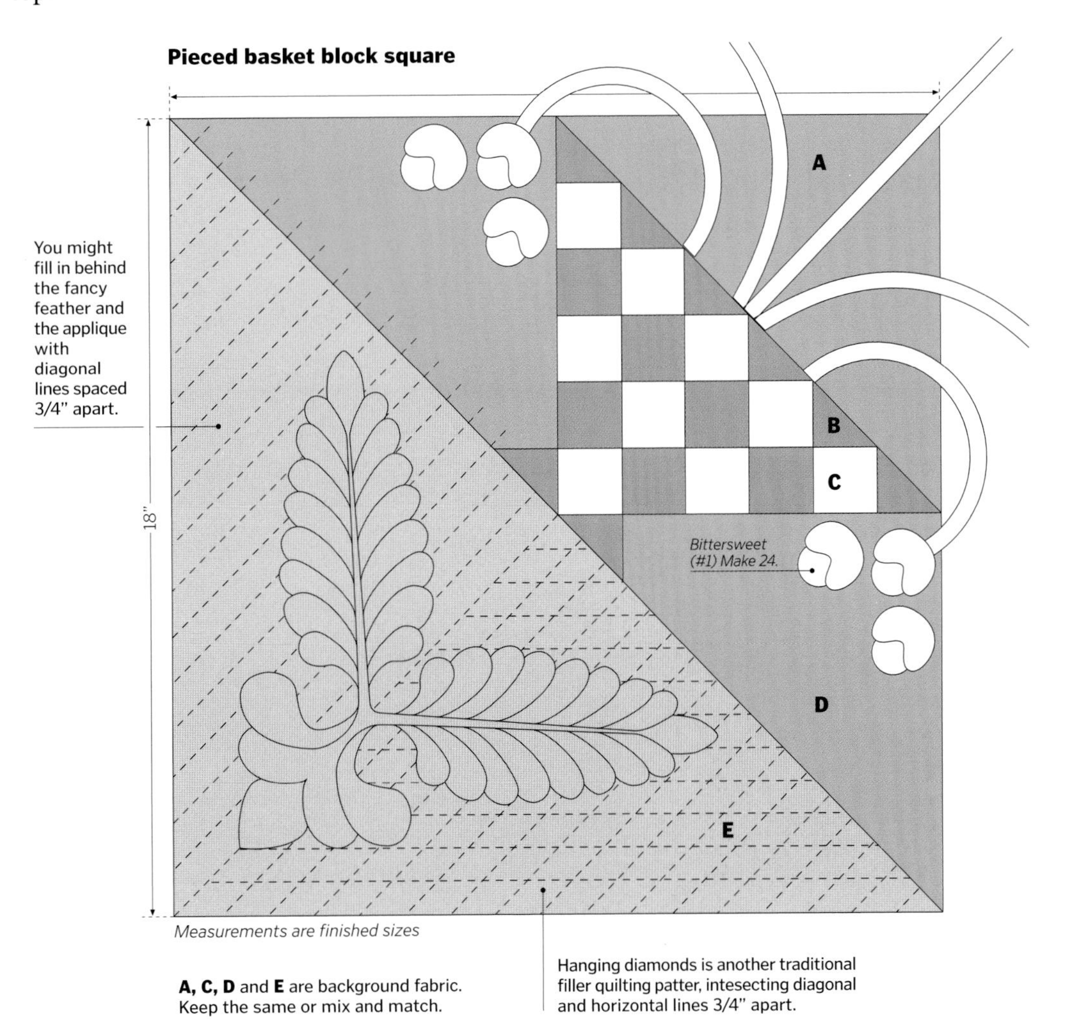

Quilting

One traditional way to quilt the appliquéd wildflowers in the blocks and border is by using echo or outline quilting. Trace the outline of the appliqué leaves, stems and flowers about **1/4**" away with a line of quilting. Then outline a second time, a half inch away and a third. You can continue this outlining right up to the seam of the block if you like. Add a little detail in the flowers and leaves by quilting circles in the centers of the flowers and veins in the leaves and petals.

A second traditional quilting pattern is to outline the appliqué one time and then fill in the rest of the block with diagonal lines about one inch or less apart. (See page 85.)

If you have included the sawtooth border you could outline-quilt each triangle, or for faster quilting, stitch a line right down the center of the strip of triangles.

Feather & Fleur-de-Lis Pattern

There is an area perfect for a fancy quilting design in the large triangle in the corner baskets. I adapted a feather with a fleur-de-lis corner from Rose Kretsinger's famous quilting designs. Rose was a master quilt designer in Emporia, Kan., in the 1930s.

This feather can also be adapted for the plain border on the rectangular quilt. Mark the corner design in each of the four corners. Find the center point of each border. Mark a series of feather designs with the feathers growing out of the corners and meeting at the center point in each border. The feathers are about 9" long so you should be able to fit eight feathers on each 72" side and six on the 54" top and bottom.

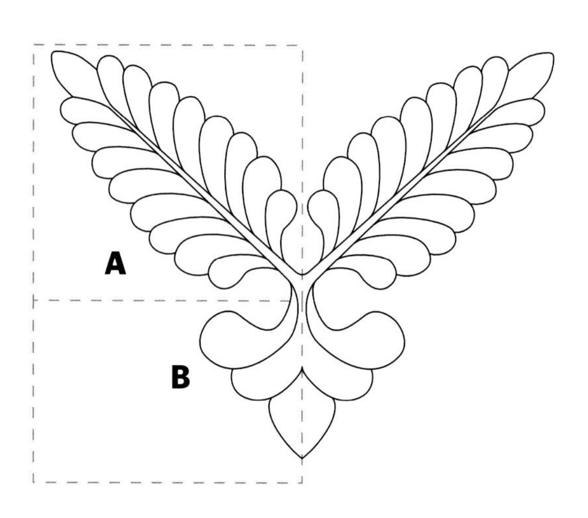

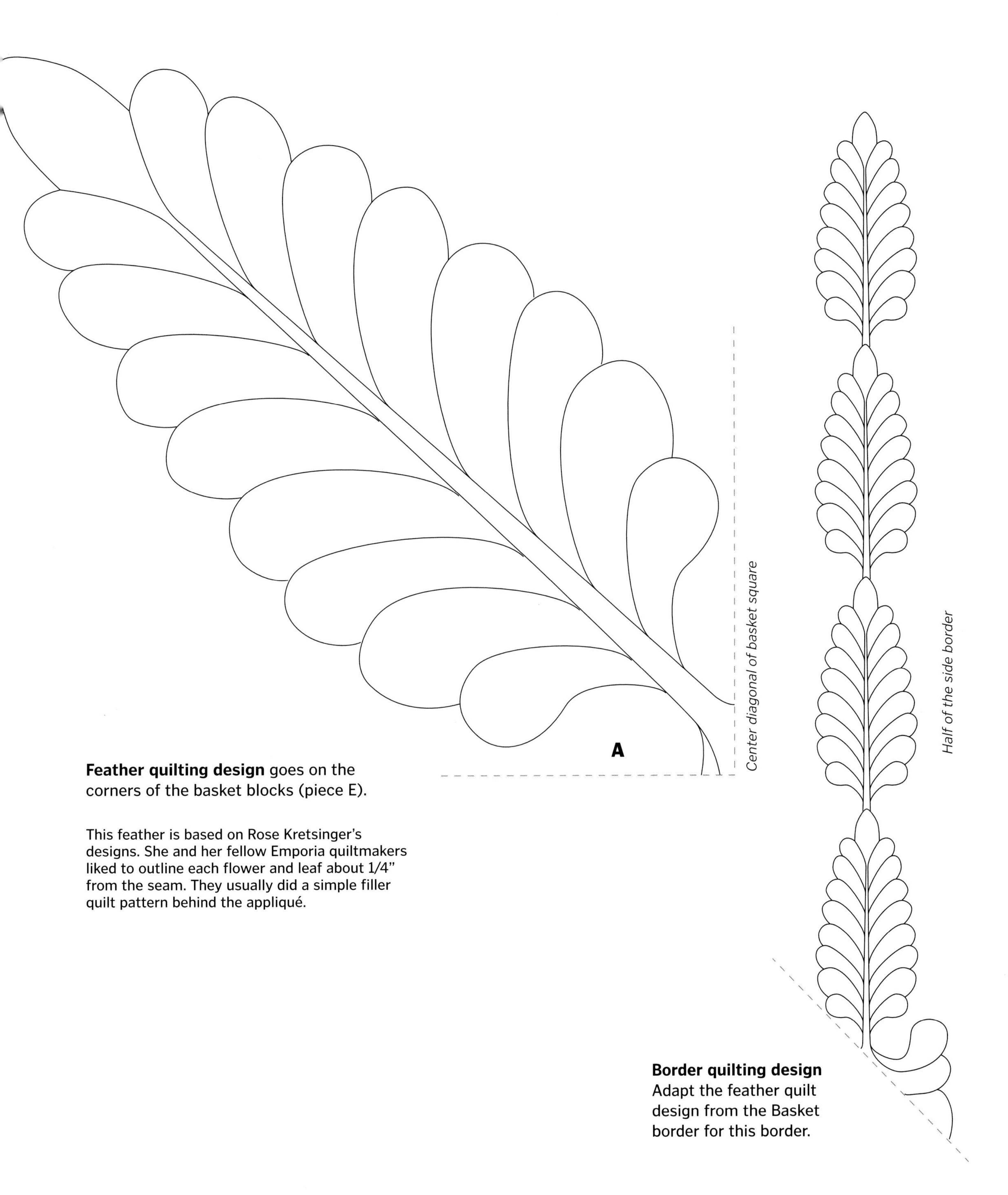

Feather quilting design goes on the corners of the basket blocks (piece E).

This feather is based on Rose Kretsinger's designs. She and her fellow Emporia quiltmakers liked to outline each flower and leaf about 1/4" from the seam. They usually did a simple filler quilt pattern behind the appliqué.

Border quilting design
Adapt the feather quilt design from the Basket border for this border.

Binding

We bound our quilt with straight grain binding, using a fabric a little bit darker than the border to serve as a frame for the whole quilt.

Fabric Requirements:

2/3 yard (24")

Cutting

Trim the selvages and cut 10 strips 2" wide by about 42" long. Piece these into four strips 90" long.

Sewing

Press the strips in half lengthwise. On the machine, stitch the folded fabric with the right sides showing to the front of your quilt. Be sure the raw edges of the binding run along the raw edges of the quilt. Use a quarter inch seam allowance. Stitch the binding to the sides first. When you get to the end of the quilt, trim neatly, leaving the raw edges. Turn the binding to the back of the quilt. Pin that folded edge neatly to the back.

Now add the binding to the top and bottom of the quilt. When you get to the edges leave a half inch seam allowance. Fold the top and bottom bindings to the back of the quilt. Pin in place, tucking the raw edges in the corners under. Hand stitch the binding to the back of the quilt.

Field of Flowers

Five Variations

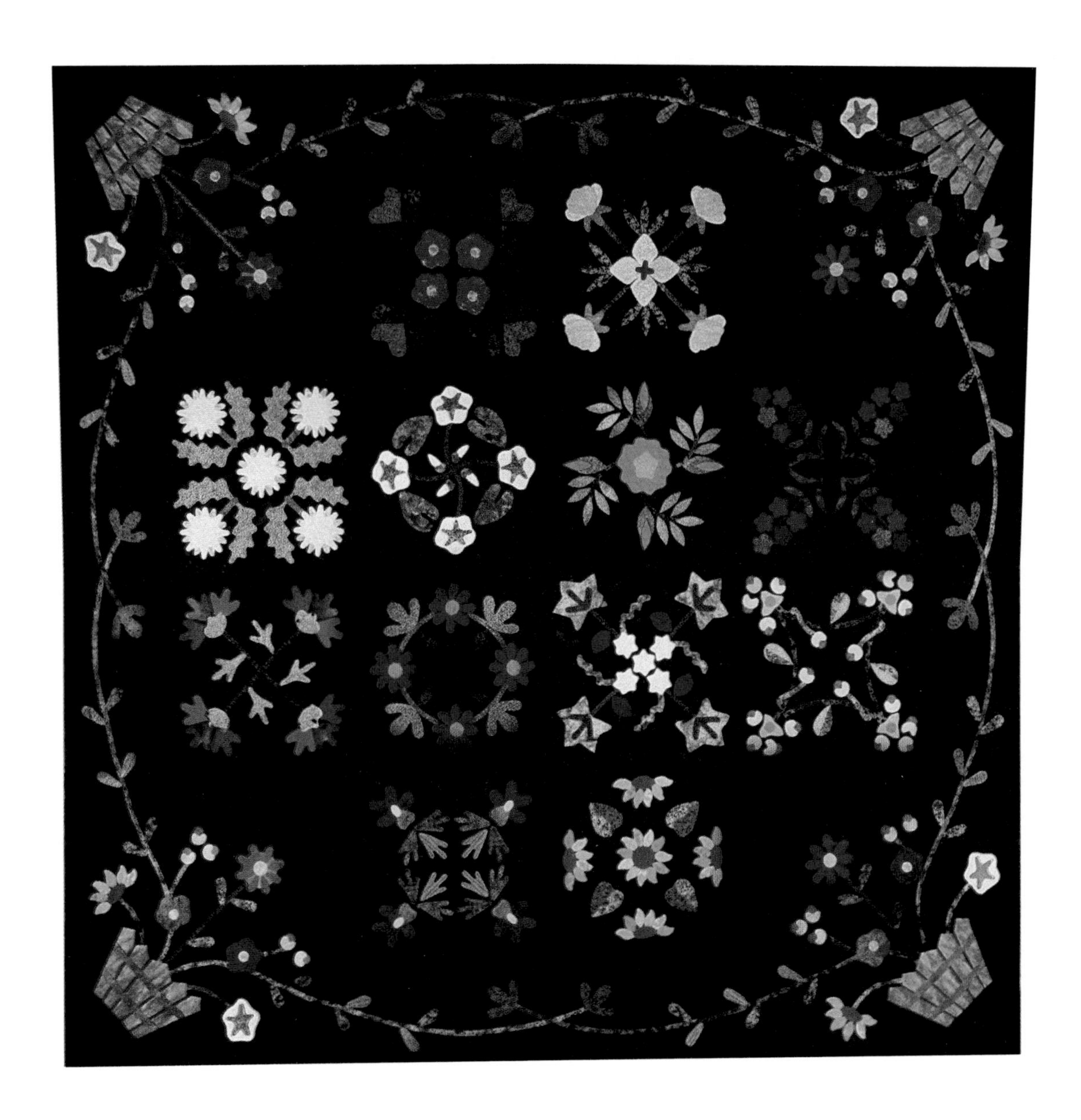

An Evening in My Garden, hand appliquéd by Linda Harker, Leavenworth, Kan., unquilted top. Linda's Leavenworth group, the Prairie Chicks, took on the Prairie Flower blocks as a design challenge. She changed quite a bit of border #3, turning the baskets 180 degrees and appliquéing garden planters instead of piecing traditional baskets.

Prairie Flower, machine appliquéd by Roseanne Smith, Lawrence, Kan., unquilted top. Roseanne embroidered the names of some of the flowers with a stem stitch. She added her own details to some of the flowers, for example, including an extra center in the dandelion.

The Prairie Is My Home, hand appliquéd by Judy Collins, Leavenworth, Kan., unquilted top. Another member of the Prairie Chicks, Judy chose a limited palette of 1930's reproduction prints and an icy white-on-white print. She added her own touch with a pieced picket fence border that Independence, Mo., artist Ruby McKim published in the 1930s and simple pieced baskets in the corners.

VICTORIAN PRAIRIE GARDEN, hand appliquéd by Denise Mariano, Leavenworth, Kan., unquilted top. Denise chose a dramatic print for the background and sashed her nine blocks for a very effective look. She designed her own flower pot for the corner and adapted four of the florals.

KANSAS FLOWERS, hand appliquéd and machine quilted by Linda Frost, Lawrence, Kan. Linda's color inspiration was the bright oriental print in the border. She used the Sawtooth border pattern (#2) and made the outside border a little bit wider than the pattern called for.

Star Quilts Year by Year

Here is a chronological list — including repeats — of the quilt patterns and designs published by The Kansas City Star from 1928 through 2001.

If you'd like to see the patterns on the pages of the newspaper, microfilm copies of The Star are available at the Kansas City Public Library's Main Branch, 311 E. 12th St., Kansas City, Mo.

For an alphabetical list of the designs, see Wilene Smith's Quilt Patterns: An Index to The Kansas City Star Patterns.

For a thumbnail sketch of each pattern, see Volume 5 of The Ultimate Illustrated Index to The Kansas City Star Quilt Pattern Collection by the Central Oklahoma Quilters Guild.

Months not listed here had no published quilt patterns.

1928

- September
  Pine Tree
  Album Quilt
- October
  French Star
  Log Cabin
  Rob Peter and Pay Paul
  Cherry Basket
  Wedding Ring
- November
  Jacob's Ladder
  Greek Cross
  Sky Rocket
  Double T
- December
  Ocean Wave
  Wild Goose Chase
  Old Maid's Puzzle
  Rambler

1929

- January
  Weathervane
  Monkey Wrench
  Spider Web
  Irish Chain
- February
  Rising Sun
  Princess Feather
  Double Nine Patch
  Eight-Pointed Star
- March
  Goose in the Pond
  Dove in the Window
  Beautiful Star
  Broken Circle
  Beggar Block
- April
  Cupid's Arrow Point
  Noon Day Lily
  Lafayette Orange Peel
  Necktie
- May
  Duck and Ducklings
  House on the Hill
  Crossed Canoes
  Turkey Tracks
- June
  Ribbon Border Block
  Posey
  Bird's Nest
  Crosses and Losses
  Double Star
- July
  Jack in the Box
  Aircraft
  Springtime Blossoms
  Sunbeam
- August
  Saw-Tooth
  Cross and Crown
  Hands All 'Round
  Honey Bee
  Flower Pot
- September
  Susannah
  Goose Tracks
  Fish Block
  Wedding Ring
- October
  Swastika
  Seth Thomas Rose
  "V" Block
  Little Beech Tree
- November
  Palm Leaf
  Tulip Appliqué
  Mill Wheel
  Order No. 11
  Old King Cole's Crown
- December
  Strawberry Block
  Old King Cole
  Little Wooden Soldier
  Road to Oklahoma
  (The "Santa's Parade Quilt" series ran in December 1929).

1930

- January
  Churn Dash
  Corn and Beans
  Rose Cross
  Milky Way
- February
  True Lovers Buggy Wheel
  Indiana Puzzle
  Blazing Star
  Aster
- March
  Sunflower
  Grape Basket
  Steps to the Altar
  Kaleidoscope
  Dutchman's Puzzle
- April
  English Flower Garden
  Single Wedding Ring
  Pin Wheels
  Cross and Crown
- May
  Missouri Puzzle
  Merry Go-Round
  Lone Star
  Missouri Star
  Sail Boat
- June
  Virginia Star
  Rail Fence
- July
  Mexican Star
  Basket of Oranges
  Rose Album
  Clay's Choice
- August
  Maple Leaf
  Sunbonnet Sue
  Compass
  Kaleidoscope
  Rainbow Tile
- September
  Goblet
  Calico Puzzle
  Broken Dishes
  Swallows in the Window
- October
  Secret Drawer
  Spider Web
  Marble Floor
  Pinwheel
  (The "Memory Bouquet Quilt" series ran in October 1930.)
- November
  Grandmother's Favorite
  Indian Emblem
  Friendship
  Puss in the Corner
  Sage-Bud
  (The "Memory Bouquet Quilt" series ran in November 1930).
- December
  Turnabout "T"
  Snow Crystals
  Sweet Gum Leaf
  Rose Dream

1931

- January
  Silver and Gold
  Tennessee Star
  Flower Pot
  Greek Cross
  Sheep Fold
- February
  Amethyst
  Wheel of Mystery
  Pontiac Star
  Baby Bunting
- March
  Seven Stars
  Rebecca's Fan
  French Bouquet
  Casement Window
- April
  Basket of Lilies
  King's Crown
  June Butterfly
  Fence Row
- May
  Indian Trail
  English Ivy
  Jackson Star
  Dutch Tulip
  Love Ring
- June
  Ararat
  Iris Leaf
  Ozark Diamond
  Kite Quilt
- July
  Cactus Flower
  Arrowhead Star
  Giddap
  Sugar Loaf
- August
  Cross Roads
  Bachelor's Puzzle
  Morning Star
  Pineapple Quilt
  Dresden Plate
- September
  Stepping Stones
  Tennessee Star
  Chips and Whetstones
  Boutonniere
- October
  Prickly Pear
  Castle Wall
  Butterfly
  Pickle Dish
  Dutch Tile
- November
  Cottage Tulips
  Formosa Tea Leaf
  Bridge
  Evening Star
- December
  Poinsettia
  Goldfish
  Christmas Star
  Crazy Daisy

1932

- January
  Friendship Knot
  Circular Saw
  Heart's Desire
  Job's Tears
  Necktie
  (The "Horn of Plenty Quilt" series also ran in January 1932).

Index of Patterns

Index of Patterns

Index of Patterns

Index of Patterns

Index of Patterns

More to read: In their own words

I commenced reading diaries of women in the West to see what role quilts played in their lives. I quickly became addicted to living in the past. One of my great delights is meeting a new friend through her diaries or letters.

I've learned much about nineteenth-century fashion, food and language (a favorite term is "commenced," which we never use anymore). I've also learned from these long-ago women ways to deal with tragedy, loss, depression and the perfidy of others. While recipes to make biscuits might change, human nature doesn't seem to.

Below are the references for each of the quotations in the book. Many are from the excellent series edited by Kenneth L. Holmes, called *Covered Wagon Women: Diaries and Letters from the Western Trails.* For years Holmes collected first person accounts and published them in 10 volumes organized by year of the journey. The series was originally published by the A. H. Clark Company. Recently, the University of Nebraska press republished the volumes in paperback under their Bison Books imprint.

Ho for California! edited by Sandra L Myres (San Marino, California: Huntington Library, 1980), collects five long accounts from manuscripts in the Henry E. Huntington Library, a great repository of western history.

Another good source for women's words are the regional and state history journals, especially *Kansas History,* which has long been committed to publishing women's as well as men's diaries and letters.

A few more books about real life on the Great Plains:

Henriette Giesberg Bruns, *Hold Dear As Always: A German Immigrant Life in Letters*, edited by Adolph E Scroeder and Carla Schulz-Geisberg, Columbia: University of Missouri Press, 1988. Gette was one of Missouri's many German settlers. Her letters back home describe Eastern Missouri through foreign eyes.

Martha Farnsworth, *Plains Woman: The Diary of Martha Farnsworth 1882-1922*, edited by Marlene Springer and Haskell Springer (Bloomington: Indiana University Press, 1986). Martha lived most of her life in Topeka.

Emily French, Emily: *The Diary of a Hard-Worked Woman*, edited by Janet Lecompte (Lincoln: University of Nebraska, 1987. Emily, a 47-year-old divorcee, lived in eastern Colorado.

Emily Hawley Gillespie, *A Secret to be Buried: The Diary and Life of Emily Hawley Gillespie*, edited by Jody Nolte Lensink (Iowa City: University of Iowa Press, 1989). Emily spent most of her life near Manchester, Iowa. She mentioned sewing and quilts quite a bit.

Elisabeth Koren, *The Diary of Elisabeth Koren, 1853-1854*, edited and translated by David T. Nelson (Northfield, Minn.: Norwegian-American Historical Association, 1955). Elisabeth was a Danish immigrant who lived near Decorah, Iowa.

References

Abbie Bright (Johnny Jump-Up) *Roughing It on Her Kansas Claim: The Diary of Abbie Bright, 1870-1871."* Edited by Joseph W. Snell, Kansas Historical Quarterly Volume XXXVI, Numbers 3 and 4, Autumn and Winter, 1971.

Harriet Talcott Buckingham (Wild Morning Glory) *Crossing the Plains in 1851.* Covered Wagon Women: Diaries and Letters from the Western Trails,1851, Volume 3. Kenneth L. Holmes, Editor. (Lincoln: University of Nebraska Bison Books, 1996).

Helen Carpenter (introduction) *Ho for California!* edited by Sandra L Myres (San Marino, Calif.: Huntington Library, 1980).

Emily Isabelle Combes (introduction) Manuscript Letters, Kansas Collection, Spencer Research Library, University of Kansas.

Clara Conron (Johnny Jump-Up) Manuscript Diary of Clara Conron, Kansas Center for Historical Research.

Elizabeth Ann Cooley (introduction) *From Virginia to Missouri in 1846: The Journal of Elizabeth Ann Cooley.* Edited by Edward D. Jervey and James E. Moss, Missouri Historical Review, 1966, Volume LX, Number 2. Pages 162-208.

Elizabeth Crawford (introduction) Letter to William H. Herndon in *The Hidden Lincoln.* Edited by Emanuel Hertz (New York: Viking Press, 1938) page 294.

Mariett Foster Cummings, (introduction) in *Covered Wagon Women: Diaries and Letters from the Western Trails, 1852, Volume 4.* Kenneth L. Holmes, Editor. (Lincoln: University of Nebraska Bison Books, 1995).

Tamsen Donner (Missouri Primrose) "The Donner Party Letters" in *Covered Wagon Women: Diaries and Letters from the Western Trails, 1840-1849, Volume 1.* Kenneth L. Holmes, Editor. (Lincoln: University of Nebraska Bison Books, 1995).

Abigail Scott Duniway, (introduction) in *Covered Wagon Women: Diaries and Letters from the Western Trails, 1852, Volume 5.* Kenneth L. Holmes, Editor. (Lincoln: University of Nebraska Bison Books, 1997).

Sarah Everett (Wood Sorrel and Indian Paintbrush) *"Letters of John and Sarah Everett."* Kansas Historical Quarterly, Volume VIII, 1939.

Amelia Hammond Hadley (Wild Rose) "Journal of Travails to Oregon: Amelia Hadley" in *Covered Wagon Women: Diaries and Letters from the Western Trails, 1851, Volume 3.* Kenneth L. Holmes, Editor. (Lincoln: University of Nebraska Bison Books, 1996).

Julia Archibald Holmes (introduction), in *Covered Wagon Women: Diaries and Letters from the Western Trails, 1854-1860, Volume 7.* Kenneth L. Holmes, Editor. (Lincoln: University of Nebraska Bison Books, 1998).

Lissie Butler Hutchinson (introduction) in *Covered Wagon Women: Diaries and Letters from the Western Trails, 1853-1854, Volume 6.* Kenneth L. Holmes, Editor. (Lincoln: University of

Nebraska Bison Books, 1997).

Elizabeth Keegan (introduction) in *Covered Wagon Women: Diaries and Letters from the Western Trails, 1852, Volume 4.* Kenneth L. Holmes, Editor. (Lincoln: University of Nebraska Bison Books, 1997).

Susan Shelby Magoffin, (introduction) *Down the Santa Fe Trail and into Mexico: The Diary of Susan Shelby Magoffin*, edited by Stella Drumm, (New Haven: Yale University Press, 1926).

Martha Missouri Moore (introduction) in *Covered Wagon Women: Diaries and Letters from the Western Trails, 1854-1860, Volume 7.* Kenneth L. Holmes, Editor. (Lincoln: University of Nebraska Bison Books, 1998).

Elizabeth Myrick (introduction) in *Covered Wagon Women: Diaries and Letters from the Western Trails, 1853-1854, Volume 6.* Kenneth L. Holmes, Editor. (Lincoln: University of Nebraska Bison Books, 1997).

Lucena Parsons (Sunflower) "An Overland Honeymoon," *Covered Wagon Women: Diaries and Letters from the Western Trails, 1850, Volume 2.* Kenneth L. Holmes, Editor. (Lincoln: University of Nebraska Bison Books, 1996).

Martha S. Read (Aster) "A History of Our Journey," in *Covered Wagon Women: Diaries and Letters from the Western Trails, 1852, Volume 5.* Kenneth L. Holmes, Editor. (Lincoln: University of Nebraska Bison Books, 1997).

Sara T. D. Robinson (Bittersweet). Sara Robinson's diary was first published in 1856 as *Kansas: Its Interior & Exterior Life*. She wrote it as a political plea for the Free-State cause and the book went through many editions. It's out of print but you may be able to find one in a library or used book source.

Elsie Snow (Dandelion) *North Central Kansas in 1887-1889: From the Letters of Leslie and Susan Snow of Junction City.* Lela Barnes, editor. Kansas Historical Quarterly Volume XXIX, # 3 & 4, 1963.

Luna Warner (Wood Sorrel and Sunflower) *The Diary of Luna E. Warner, a Kansas Teenager of the Early 1870's.* Venola Lewis Bivans, editor. Kansas Historical Quarterly, Volume XXXV, August, 1969.

Ella S. Wells (introduction) "Letters of a Kansas Pioneer," *Kansas Historical Quarterly, Volume V*, 1936.

Laura Ingalls Wilder (Sweet William) Laura Ingalls Wilder and Rose Wilder Lane, *A Little House Sampler*. Edited by William T. Anderson. (Lincoln: University of Nebraska Press, 1989).

Caroline Frey Winne (Wild Cucumber) "Letters of Caroline Frey Winne from Sidney Barracks and Fort McPherson, Nebraska, 1874-1878." Thomas R. Buecher, editor. *Nebraska History. Volume LXII, Number 1.* Spring, 1981.